LOG CABIN

WITH

A

TWIST

LOG CABIN

WITH

A

TWIST

by
Barbara T. Kaempfer

American Quilter's Society
P. O. Box 3290 • Paducah, KY 42002-3290

Library of Congress Cataloging-in-Publication Data

Kaempfer, Barbara
    Log cabin with a twist/ by Barbara Kaempfer.
        p.   cm.
    ISBN 0-89145 -855-7
     1. Patchwork -- Patterns.   2. Log cabin quilts   I. Title.
TT835.K33   1995
  746.46--dc20   95--34081
                                             CIP

Additional copies of this book may be ordered from:

American Quilter's Society
P.O. Box 3290
Paducah, KY 42002-3290
@18.95. Add $2.00 for postage and handling.

Printed by IMAGE GRAPHICS, INC., Paducah, Kentucky

Dedication

To my husband Ueli, my daughter Sabine, and my son Gregor.

Acknowledgments

To Sonja Shogren, the person who first introduced me to quilting.

To Jane Hall, my first quilting teacher who taught me the basics.

To all the other teachers sharing their knowledge and showing me new ways to create beautiful quilts.

To Mary Ellen Hopkins for inspiring me to write this book.

To all my students that have ever been in my classes and asked many questions, challenging me over and over again.

To all the students that share their gorgeous quilts in this book.

To my husband Ueli who helped me find a way to write this book and is always supportive and encouraging.

All photos in the book are taken by Foto Studio Steiner in Affoltern am Albis, Switzerland.

Contents

Preface

When I first discovered the twisted Log Cabin pattern some years ago, I knew immediately that I was going to be captivated by this for a long time.

The twisted Log Cabin technique has some similarities with the traditional Log Cabin:

- there are thousands of possibilities
- one block alone may not be very impressive
- a quilt should be made of four blocks at least
- quilts of six blocks or more make even more interesting designs.

Although I have experimented with different shapes for some time now, I still haven't found a limitation to the number of possibilities. After I finished my first twisted Log Cabin quilts, everyone seemed curious about the technique. Obviously there is a significant need to teach this new technique and to share the fun with fellow quilters. At my semi-annual Quilt-Seminar in fall 1990 in Unterägeri (Switzerland) I taught this new technique for the first time and have done so regularly since. During one of those seminars Mary Ellen Hopkins suggested that I write a book about it. "Me? Write a book?" This appeared to be an impossible task at first.

This book is the result of a combination of efforts undertaken over a long period of time. It explains how to approach the twisted Log Cabin technique. There are many examples illustrating some of the possibilities.

I certainly hope you'll enjoy working with this pattern and technique as much as I do. The resulting designs and quilts are definitely worth the effort.

Introduction

HOW TO USE THIS BOOK

Chapter 1, The Square; Chapter 2, The Equilateral Triangle; and Chapter 3, The 90° Triangle, tell you:
- how to draw the basic blocks for the twisted Log Cabin pattern
- how to assemble and color them, resulting in design examples.

For these parts you just work with paper, pencil, ruler, and colors. To do your coloring you may use colored pencils, watercolors, or felt-tip pens. Use the tools you are most comfortable with.

For your convenience this book contains many ready-to-use drawings in the appendices. You should make photocopies of them to be used for your personal coloring exercises. In this way you may use them many times over.

Chapter 4 explains how to draw other shapes and how to combine different shapes into one design.

Chapter 5 guides you through the actual making of the quilt.

Even if these patterns seem complicated at first, don't worry! By following the instructions in this book, step by step, you'll soon realize that it is not difficult at all. There are no mathematics (other than adding numbers) required.

I have not included any hints about materials used in quilting because I'm sure you know for yourself what materials you like best to work with. There is no color theory either because I think this is a separate subject.

I wrote this book in English (although my mother tongue is German) mainly because it is the language of the largest community of quilters. I used American measurements (inch) because the book was published in the U.S. Also, I personally prefer to work with inches, but in my classes I give my students all the measurements in centimeters, too.

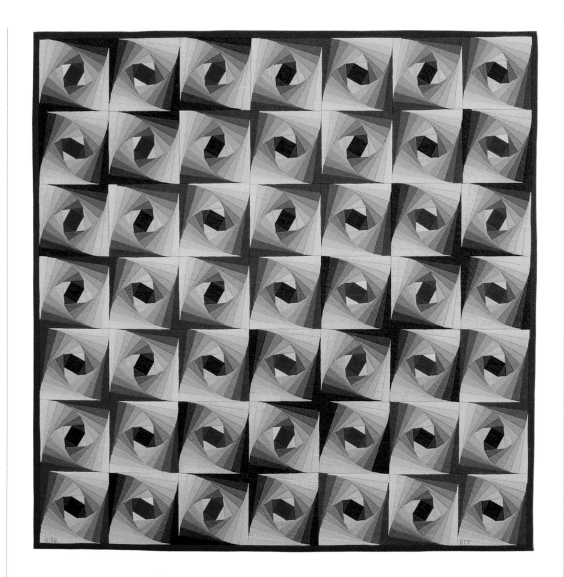

The Square

This chapter guides you through the drawing and designing steps to create a twisted Log Cabin pattern based on a square.

HOW TO DRAW THE PATTERN

To draw all of the patterns in this book you need a C-Thru™ (see-through) ruler and a pencil or set of colored pencils. Keep the pencils well sharpened at all times. It is important to work accurately from the beginning – small mistakes add up quickly!

BLOCK SIZE

As usual, before you start a new quilt project you have to decide what block size you want to work with. All of the examples in this chapter are based on a square with a 6" side length. You may decide to use a different size, but then you will need to recalculate the measurements given in this chapter. Therefore, for your first design I strongly recommend that you use the same 6" block.

ADDING TWIST

The second decision you have to make is how much *twist* you want in your pattern. The result of this decision is a unit of measurement that is a fraction of the side length of your block. In this chapter the measurement used is ¾" (this is an eighth of the side length of your block).

It is important to note that the shorter this unit of measurement is, the more twist the pattern will show, and the more strips it will be made of.

Again, I urge you to use the ¾" measurement from the example in this chapter for your first design efforts.

DRAWING THE PATTERN

Step 1. Draw a 6" square on graph paper with preprinted cross-sections (preprinted 16 squares per square inch, also called 4 sq./in). This 6" square is called the A-square. Mark the corners of the A-square A1, A2, A3, and A4 in a clockwise direction. The example starts with the upper left corner, but you may start at any corner you like. See Figure 1.

Step 2. Starting at corner A1 measure ¾" along the line toward corner A2. Mark this point on the line. Name it B1. Repeat this step in a clockwise direction

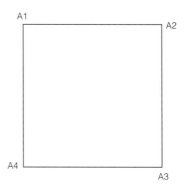

ABOVE
Figure 1. The A-square.

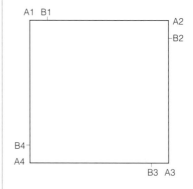

ABOVE
Figure 2. A-square with marked corners of B-square.

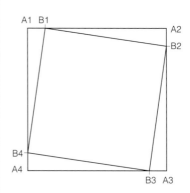

ABOVE
Figure 3. B-square inside A-square.

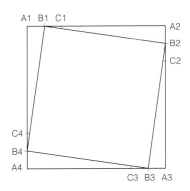

ABOVE

Figure 4. A- and B-square with marked corners of C-square.

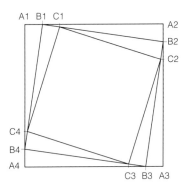

ABOVE

Figure 5. A-, B-, and C-square.

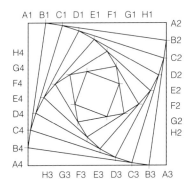

ABOVE

Figure 6. A–H-square when completed.

for the line between A2 and A3. Mark this point B2. Repeat this step in a clockwise direction for lines A3 and A4, and A4 and A1. Mark the resulting points B3 and B4 respectively. See Figure 2.

Step 3. Using a different color pencil, connect the B-points with straight lines: B1 with B2, B2 with B3, etc. The result is a smaller, rotated square with its corners touching the lines of your A-square. This smaller square is called the B-square. See Figure 3. By using a different color pencil for each square, it may be easier to verify that you really finished every square. It is advisable to use rather dark colors that are well suited for photocopying. This will be convenient when you want to duplicate your drawings with a photocopier.

Step 4. Now measure and mark ¾" from the B-points along the B-lines in a clockwise direction, producing the points C1, C2, C3, and C4. See Figure 4.

Step 5. Connect the C-points to get the C-square. The C-square is even smaller than the B-square, it is rotated, and its corners touch the lines of your B-square. See Figure 5.

Step 6. Repeat steps 4 and 5 until you have seven squares (B – H) in your 6" A-square. See Figure 6.

It is very important to work in a precise manner.

You have now completed the drawing of the basic block. If you have done everything correctly, the result of your work should look exactly like Appendix A1.

OTHER BLOCK SIZES AND MEASUREMENTS

The following table shows some useful proportions for blocks of different sizes:

Side length of the block	Unit of measurement for twist
8 inches	1", ⅞", or ¾"
6 inches	¾", ⅝", or ½"
4 inches	½", ⅜", or ¼"
2 inches	¼" or ⅜"

I suggest you try other proportions as well.

COMBINING BLOCKS INTO A DESIGNS (ON PAPER)

As with the traditional Log Cabin pattern, a single block might not be very impressive. Let's see what happens when we put several identical blocks together.

You need to make four photocopies of the block you just finished drawing. You'll need these to experiment with the possible combinations; your original block can be saved for future use.

REDUCING THE DESIGN AND COLORING EFFORT

During the paper design phase you will do a lot of coloring with colored pencils. Using reduced copies of the original 6" design saves both time and effort.

To make reductions of the original design you can:
- make photocopies on a copier that has a reduction feature
- draw the pattern again with smaller measurements and photocopy it
- make copies of the reduced designs in Appendix A2.

As the owner of this book you can make as many copies of the figures in this book as you want for your personal use.

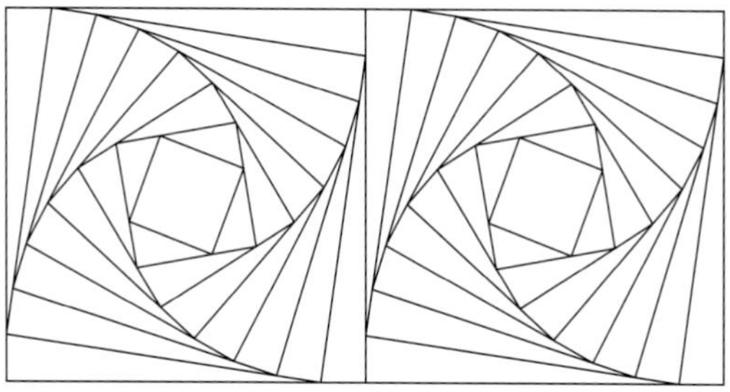

COMBINING TWO BLOCKS AND COLORING

Step 1. Cut out the blocks along the outer edge of the borderline of the A-square.

Step 2. Put two blocks adjacent to each other to form a rectangle. See Figure 7.

Step 3. A new shape becomes visible across the joining borders of the blocks that I call the twisted ribbon. See Figure 8.

In this example, the twisted ribbon is made up of a total of 14 sharply pointed triangles, seven pointing down, seven pointing up. The individual triangle is called a strip.

As you will see, new shapes (like the twisted ribbon) that cross the borders of joined blocks are what make the twisted Log Cabin technique so exciting.

ABOVE
Figure 7. Two squares joined.

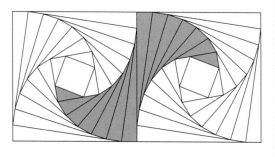

ABOVE
Figure 8. Twisted ribbon (14 strips).

Step 4. Emphasize the twisted ribbon by coloring. It is easiest to color one single block completely before replicating the same colors on the other blocks.

   a. Choose seven colors from one color range, for example, yellow to orange to red.

   b. Start by coloring one of the outermost strips with the darkest color of the range you chose.

   c. Color the outermost strip on the opposite side of the block with the same color.

   d. Color the next strip toward the center of the block with the next lighter color of the color range you chose.

   e. Repeat step 4d on the opposite side.

   f. Repeat steps 4d and 4e five more times. Leave the center square blank.

Step 5. An area made up of the center square and two opposite half-twisted ribbons is still blank. Color this band with one color value that is different from the seven colors you used so far (for example, gray). This is called background coloring. The coloring pattern used here is similar to the Courthouse Steps in traditional Log Cabin design. See Figure 9.

Step 6. Repeat the coloring (steps 4b – 4f and 5) on the second block with the same colors.

Step 7. Rejoin the two colored blocks as you did in Step 2.

The twisted ribbon reappears with the darkest colored strips forming the center of the twisted ribbon. You have two halves of a twisted ribbon on each side of the rectangle as well. See Figure 10.

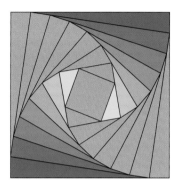

ABOVE
Figure 9. Single square colored.

COMBINING FOUR AND MORE BLOCKS INTO DIFFERENT DESIGNS

Repeat coloring with the same colors for the third and fourth block. After that you should have four identical blocks.

Join blocks 3 and 4 the same way you did blocks 1 and 2.

Join the two rectangles to form a Four-Patch. This is one of several possible combinations, resulting in the first design. See Figure 11, next page.

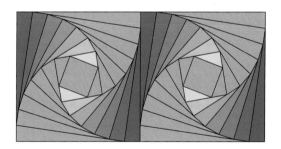

ABOVE
Figure 10. Two joined squares colored, forming a ribbon.

ABOVE
Figure 11. Four-Patch colored, first design.

Combining the same four blocks in another way results in a second design. This is achieved by turning the upper right and lower left blocks by 90° (a quarter turn) in the same direction. Since the blocks are symmetrical it doesn't matter which way you turn them. See Figure 12.

The four strips touching at the center of the Four-Patch are all of the darkest color you chose.

If you turn the upper left and lower right blocks instead of the other two, the four strips that meet at the center of the Four-Patch will be of the background color. This only matters if you do not enlarge your design by more than four blocks. If you do join more (for example, sixteen) blocks, the same pattern as in Figure 13 will reappear.

Again, this shows that it usually takes at least four blocks to make an interesting design visible. See Figure 12.

When you are pleased with your design make it permanent by gluing the blocks on a sheet of paper. See Figure 14.

ABOVE
Figure 12. Four-Patch colored, second design.

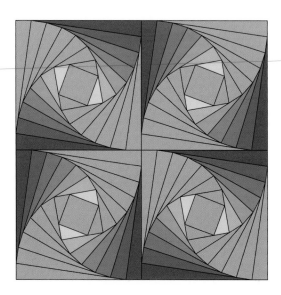

ABOVE
Figure 13. Four-Patch colored.

Figure 14. Sixteen-Patch colored, third design.

DIFFERENT DESIGNS USING THE SAME PATTERN AND COLORS

The simplest way to get a different effect of the design is by using the colors in reversed order. Do steps 4a – 5 (see section Combining Two Blocks and Coloring on page 14) on a fresh set of blocks, but this time start with the lightest color of the range you chose and finish with the darkest. Appendix A2 is intended for coloring single blocks, cutting them out and arranging them in designs. This allows you to try different arrangements by re-using the same blocks. Appendix A3 is intended for coloring designs without cutting them out. Use whichever technique suits you best. See Figure 15, next page.

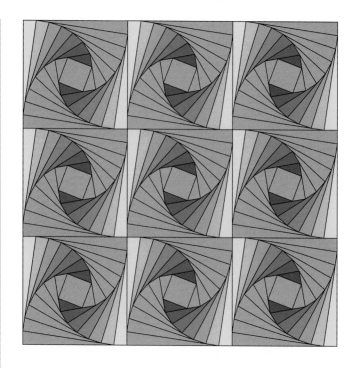

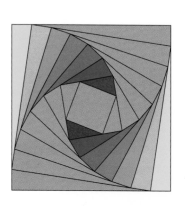

ABOVE & RIGHT
Figure 15. Single square and Nine-Patch colored, light to dark on both sides.

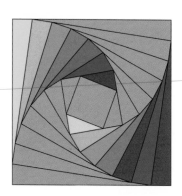

ABOVE & RIGHT
Figure 16. Single square and Nine-Patch colored, light to dark on one side, dark to light on the other side.

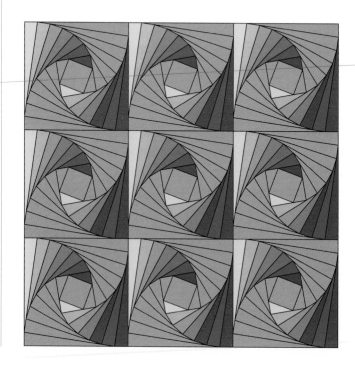

Another simple way to change the appearance of the design is by using the colors in reversed order only on one side of the block. See Figure 16.

The next version of the design uses one additional color for the center square. The center square now connects the two halves of the twisted ribbon and is no longer part of the background. See Figure 17.

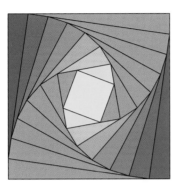

LEFT & BELOW
Figure 17. Single square and Nine-Patch colored, center square connecting.

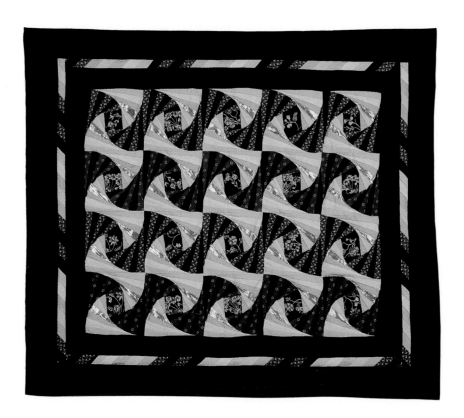

Plate 2. WELLEN, 1992,
32" x 28" (80cm x 70cm).
Ruth von Arx, Küsnacht,
Switzerland.

RIGHT
Plate 3. GRINDELWALD 1,
1994, 19" x 19" (48cm x 48cm).
Barbara T. Kaempfer,
Mettmenstetten, Switzerland.

Plate 4. GRINDELWALD 2,
1994, 19" x 19" (48cm x 48cm).
Barbara T. Kaempfer,
Mettmenstetten, Switzerland,
owned by Mr. and Mrs.
Luchsinger, Horgen,
Switzerland.

Plate 5. GRINDELWALD 3,
1994, 19" x 19" (48cm x 48cm).
Barbara T. Kaempfer,
Mettmenstetten, Switzerland,
owned by Mr. and Mrs.
Luchsinger, Horgen,
Switzerland.

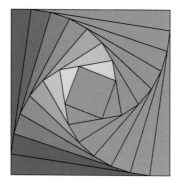

ABOVE
Figure 18. Single square colored.

BELOW
*Figure 19. Nine-Patch colored,
Straight Furrows.*

MORE DESIGN POSSIBILITIES USING THE SAME PATTERN AND COLORS

The designs that follow are similar to Light and Dark block arrangements in traditional Log Cabin quilts.

Another striking design can be achieved by coloring two half ribbons next to each other (instead of opposite) on a block. Start by coloring the left most and the bottom strip with the same darkest color of the range you chose. Continue coloring the strips from the left and bottom towards the center using the color range from earlier examples. Color the rest of the block (including the center) with the background color. See Figure 18.

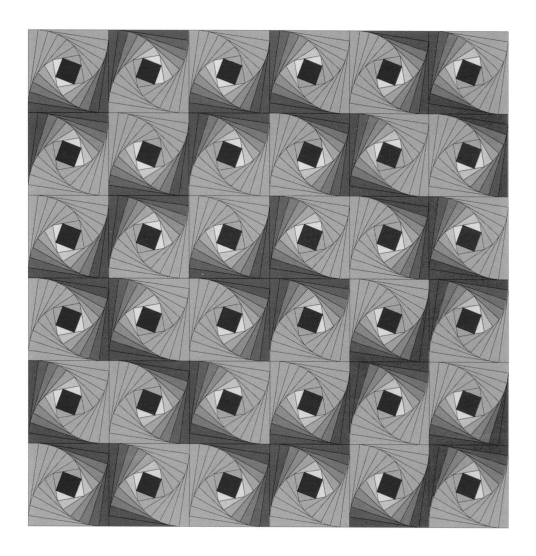

ABOVE
Figure 20. Barn Raising.

Color another eight blocks (total of nine) exactly the same way. Put the nine blocks together to produce a design similar to the traditional Straight Furrows design. See Figure 19, page 22. If you are still in the mood do another 27 identical blocks (total of 36; use copies of Appendix A3). Arrange them to achieve a design similar to the Barn Raising arrangement. See Figure 20, page 23. Most of the traditional Log Cabin designs may be used for the twisted Log Cabin technique – they just look different. Here are some other examples: Figures 21 and 22 and Plates 6 through 9, pages 26 through 29.

BELOW
Figure 21.

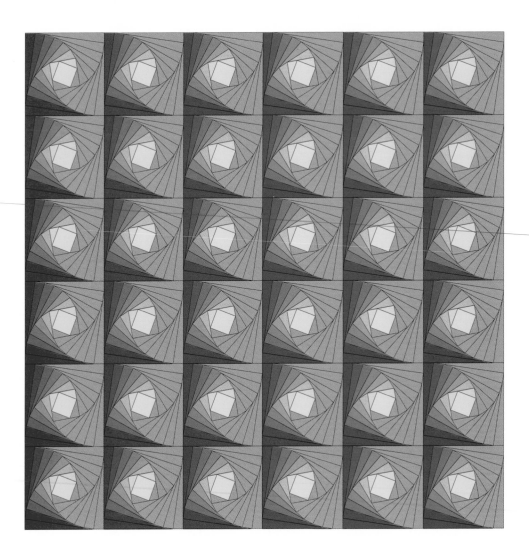

24

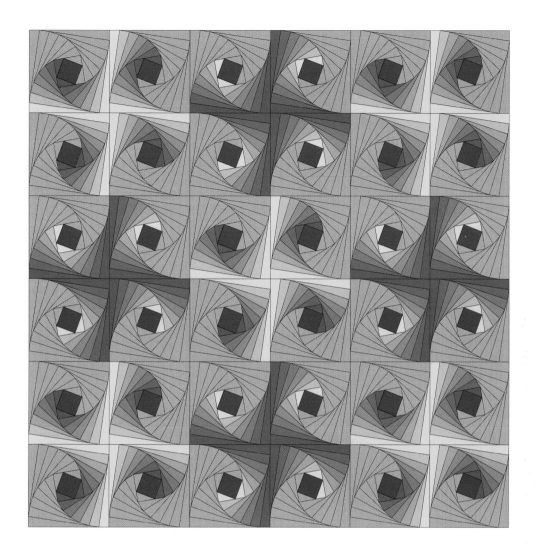

ABOVE
Figure 22. Light and Dark.

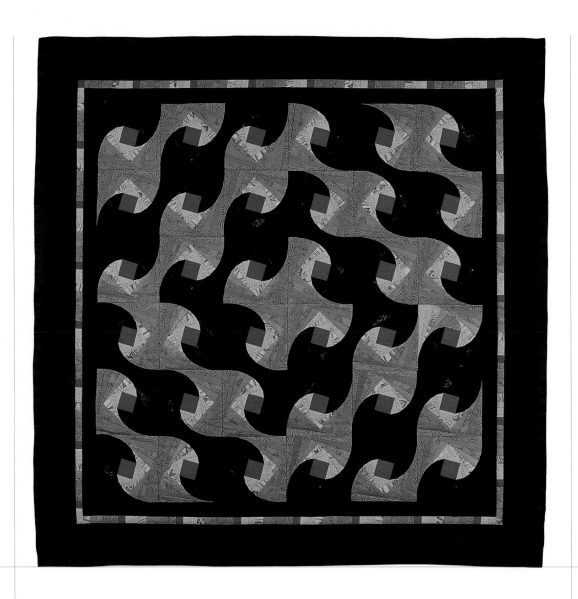

ABOVE
Plate 6. BLACK AND GREY,
1993, 38" x 38" (95cm x 95cm).
Regula Emmenegger,
Gümligen, Switzerland.

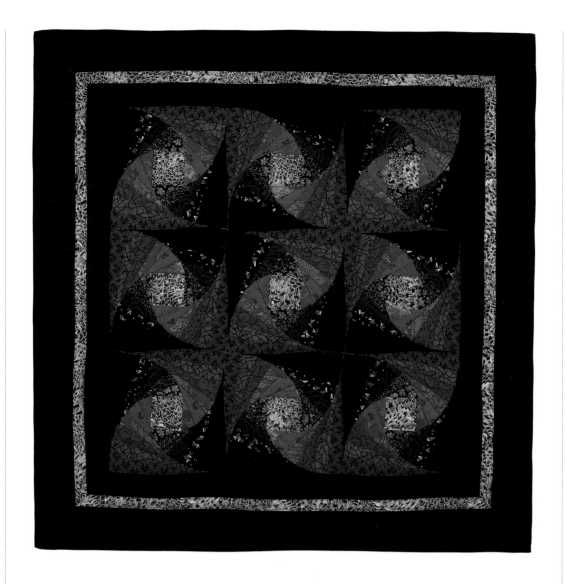

*Plate 7. FEUER (Fire), 1994,
26" x 26" (65cm x 65cm).
Esther Kronenberg, Langnau
am Albis, Switzerland.*

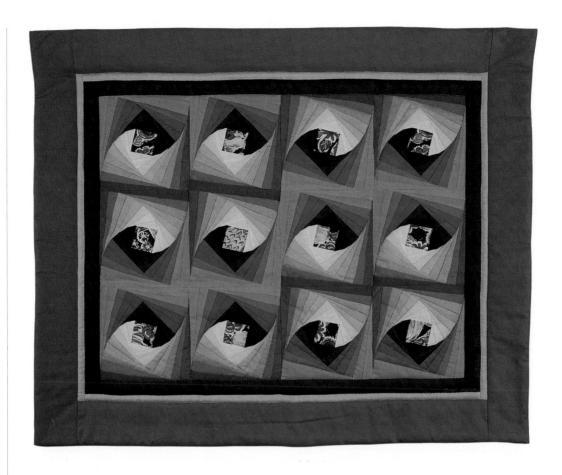

Plate 8. WELLEN (Waves),
1993, 40" x 34" (100cm x
85cm). Angelika Meier,
Dällikon, Switzerland.

Plate 9. SUNRISE AND SUNSET, 1993, 26" x 26" (66cm x
66cm). Käthy Gubler, Hirzel, Switzerland. Two quilt set.

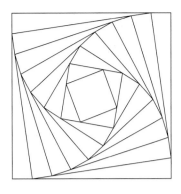

ABOVE
*Figure 23. Single block with a
counterclockwise twist.*

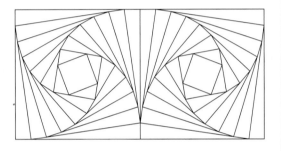

ABOVE
*Figure 24. Two blocks joined to
create a "fan."*

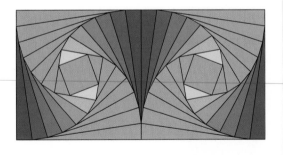

ABOVE
*Figure 25. Two colored blocks
joined.*

RIGHT
Figure 26. Nine-Patch colored.

MIRROR IMAGE DESIGNS

With the twisted Log Cabin technique countless designs are possible that are similar to the traditional Log Cabin. But the twisted Log Cabin technique allows even more combinations by reversing the twist on some of the blocks used in a design. This is also called a mirror image.

To draw a mirror image block, do steps 1 – 6 as described in How to Draw the Pattern on page 12, but instead of measuring in a clockwise direction you now measure in a counterclockwise direction. See Figure 23. If you have done everything correctly, the result should look like Appendix A4.

For the following steps use copies of Appendices A2 (clockwise blocks) and A5 (counterclockwise blocks). Cut out one block with clockwise pattern and one block with a counterclockwise pattern. Put the two blocks side by side. A new shape emerges across the two blocks; I call it a "fan." See Figure 24.

Color the strips of the fan on one clockwise block (as described in Combining Blocks into Design, steps 4 – 5 on page 15) using the same colors. Repeat the coloring on a counterclockwise block (same colors). Join the two blocks. See Figure 25.

Produce seven more blocks to combine them into a Nine-Patch. See Figure 26.

By using the colors in reversed order you get another unique design, although the underlying pattern remains the same. See Figures 27 and 28.

Changing the center square yields still another interesting design possibility. See Figure 29.

A further range of design possibilities emerges by coloring the single blocks similarly to the traditional Log Cabin Light and Dark (see Plate 39, page 81). See Figure 30 and Plates 10 through 12, pages 32 through 34.

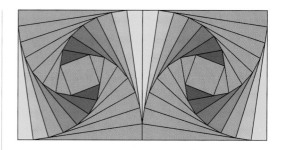

ABOVE
Figure 27. Two colored blocks joined.

LEFT
Figure 28. Nine-Patch colored.

LEFT
Figure 29. Nine-Patch colored.

BELOW
Figure 30. Two blocks colored.

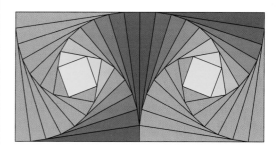

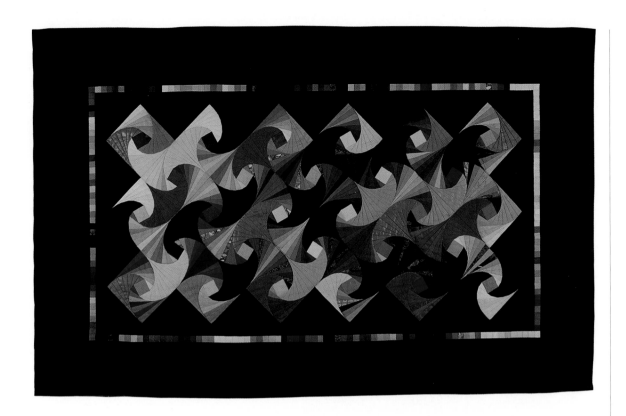

ABOVE
Plate 10. COLOR FANTASIA I,
1992, 54" x 34" (135cm x
85cm). Regula Emmenegger,
Gümligen, Switzerland.
This striking quilt is made of
clockwise and counterclock-
wise blocks, set on point, using
many different colors. The
underlying pattern is a simple
twisted square.

ABOVE
Plate 11. COLOR FANTASIA II, DANCING CLOWNS, 1994, 48" x 40" (120cm x 100cm). Regula Emmenegger, Gümligen, Switzerland.

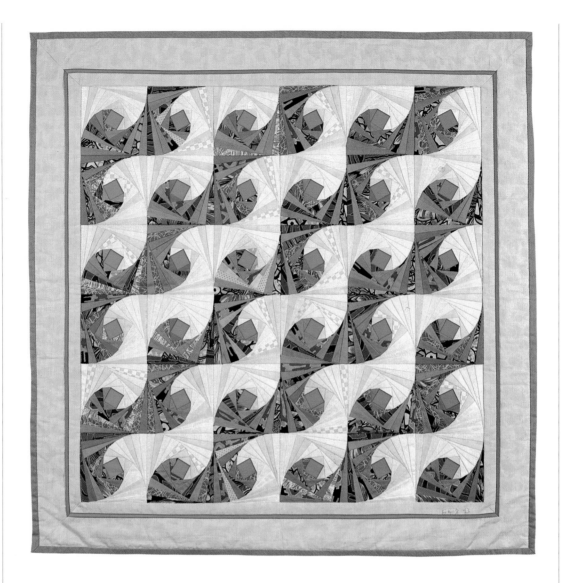

ABOVE
Plate 12. KNOSPEN (Buds),
1993, 30" x 30" (77cm x 77cm).
Barbara T. Kaempfer,
Mettmenstetten, Switzerland.
This is based on the Straight
Furrows design.

The Equilateral
Triange

The equilateral triangle is a symmetrical figure with three 60° corners and all sides equal. The following steps will help you draw and design a twisted Log Cabin pattern based on an equilateral triangle.

ABOVE
Plate 13. AQUARIUS, 1993, 28" x 24" (70cm x 60cm). Regula Emmenegger, Gümligen, Switzerland.

HOW TO DRAW THE PATTERN

To draw the pattern you need a C-thru™ ruler and a pencil or different color pencils. Remember, it is important to work very accurately right from the beginning because small mistakes add up quickly.

BLOCK SIZE

As usual, before starting a new quilt project, first you have to decide what size block you want to make. All the examples in this chapter are based on an 8" equilateral triangle. You may decide to use a different size, but you will need to recalculate all the measurements given in this chapter. Therefore, I strongly recommend you use the 8" block for your first design.

ADDING TWIST

The second decision you have to make is how much *twist* you want to have in your pattern. The result of this decision is a unit of measurement that is a fraction of the side length of your block. Again, in this chapter a ¾" measurement is used.

It is important to note that the shorter this unit of measurement is, the more twist the block will show and the more strips it will be made of. I suggest you stay with the ¾" measurement used for the example of this chapter.

There are two ways to construct an equilateral triangle:

- using a compass (to keep things simple, I won't go into explanations here)
- using paper with preprinted, small equilateral triangles.

The second method certainly is the easier one. For your convenience Appendix B1 contains such a preprinted page. Make copies of it to do your drawing on. This paper is usually available in quilt shops.

DRAWING THE PATTERN

Step 1. Draw an equilateral triangle with a side length of 8 inches. This is called the A-equilateral. Mark its corners A1, A2, and A3 in a clockwise direction. See Figure 31.

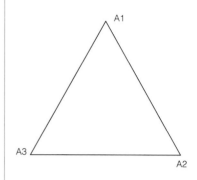

ABOVE
Figure 31. A-equilateral.

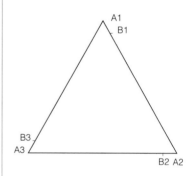

ABOVE
Figure 32. A-equilateral with marked B-points.

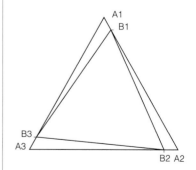

ABOVE
Figure 33. B-equilateral inside A-equilateral.

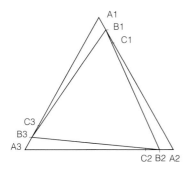

ABOVE

Figure 34. A- and B-equilateral with marked C-points.

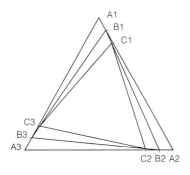

ABOVE

Figure 35. B- and C-equilateral inside A-equilateral.

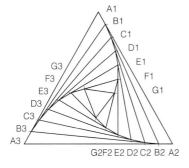

ABOVE

Figure 36. Completed equilateral.

Step 2. Starting at corner A1 measure ¾" along the line toward corner A2. Mark this point on the line. Name it B1. Repeat this step in a *clockwise* direction for the line between A2 – A3. Mark this point and name it B2. Repeat this step again for the line between A3 – A1, resulting in the mark named B3. See Figure 32.

Step 3. Connect the B-points with straight lines: B1 with B2, B2 with B3, and B3 with B1. The result is a smaller, rotated equilateral whose corners touch the lines of your A-equilateral. This smaller equilateral is called the B-equilateral. By using a different color pencil for each equilateral it may be easier for you to verify that you really have completed each equilateral. See Figure 33.

Step 4. Now measure and mark ¾" from the B-points along the B-lines in a clockwise direction, producing the points C1, C2, and C3. See Figure 34.

Step 5. Connect the C-points with straight lines to get the C-equilateral. The C-equilateral is even smaller than the B-equilateral, is rotated, and its corners touch the B-equilateral. See Figure 35.

Step 6. Repeat steps 4 and 5 until you have six smaller equilateral triangles in your 8" A-equilateral (B to G). See Figure 36. It is very important to work in a precise manner. If you have done everything correctly, the result of your work should look exactly like Appendix B2. You have now completed the drawing of the basic block with a clockwise twist.

OTHER BLOCK SIZES AND MEASUREMENTS

The following table shows some useful proportions for blocks of different sizes:

Side length of the block	Unit of measurement for twist
8 inches	1", ⅞", or ¾"
6 inches	¾", ⅝", or ½"
4 inches	½", ⅜", or ¼"

Try other proportions as well.

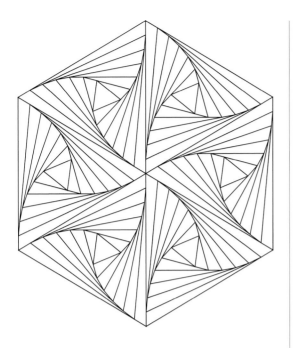

ABOVE
Figure 37. Six equilateral triangles forming a hexagon.

ABOVE
Figure 38. Twisted ribbons.

COMBINING BLOCKS INTO A DESIGN (ON PAPER)

In order to create a meaningful design you'll need to combine six blocks. For that purpose you need to make copies of the block you drew.

REDUCING THE DESIGN AND COLORING EFFORT

During the design phase you will do quite a lot of coloring with colored pencils. Coloring 8" blocks takes some effort, which can be reduced substantially if you make smaller versions of the block just for coloring. You can make reduced designs in three ways:

- make photocopies on a copying machine that has a reduction feature
- do the drawing again with a smaller A-equilateral
- make copies of the reduced designs in Appendix B3.

COMBINING SIX BLOCKS

Step 1. Cut out the blocks along the outer edge of the borderline of the A-equilateral.

Step 2. Put the six blocks together so they form a hexagon. See Figure 37.

Step 3. A new shape becomes visible across the borders of the blocks that I call the twisted ribbon. See Figure 38.

Step 4. In contrast to the square (Chapter 1), in which an individual block is completely colored before it is combined into larger designs, with the equilateral triangle it is easier first to assemble a hexagon from six blank blocks and then color the hexagon. You may use copies of Appendix B4.

- **a.** Choose six colors fitting one color range, for example purples from light to dark.
- **b.** Start by coloring the six strips touching at the center of the hexagon with the color from one end of the color range you chose. See Figure 39.
- **c.** Color the strip adjacent to the one you just did in each block with the next color in your range.

d. Color the remaining strips by working through your color range. Leave the center triangle of each of the blocks blank. See Figure 40.

e. Color the six strips that almost reach the center of the hexagon with their sharp points with the color you used last.

f. Color the adjacent strips by working through your colors in *reverse* order. This should still leave the center triangle of each of the six blocks blank.

Step 5. Color the center triangle and the remaining six strips of each of the six blocks with a different color as background (gray in this example). See Figure 41.

Figure 40. One half of the twist colored.

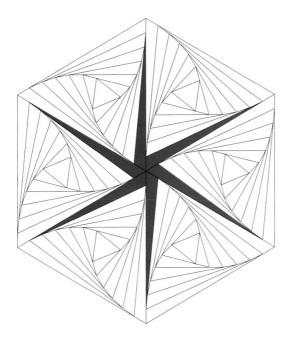

Figure 39. One strip colored.

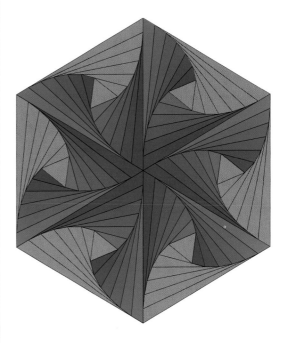

Figure 41. Twisted ribbon colored.

DIFFERENT DESIGNS USING THE SAME PATTERN AND COLORS

A very simple way of creating a different design is by coloring only half of the twisted ribbons, leaving two-thirds of each block and the center for background coloring. To achieve this, do steps 4a – 4d (step 4 on pages 38 – 39) again. Skip steps 4e – 4f, and color the center triangle and the remaining two-thirds of each of the six blocks with the background color. See Figure 42 and Plates 14 through 17, pages 40 through 42.

ABOVE
Figure 42. One half of twisted ribbon colored (flower).

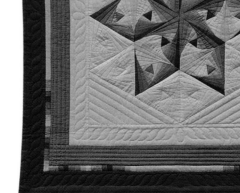

RIGHT
Plate 14. POLARSTERN (Polarstar), 1991, 42" x 44" (105cm x 110cm). Eveline Rufer, Amriswil, Switzerland.

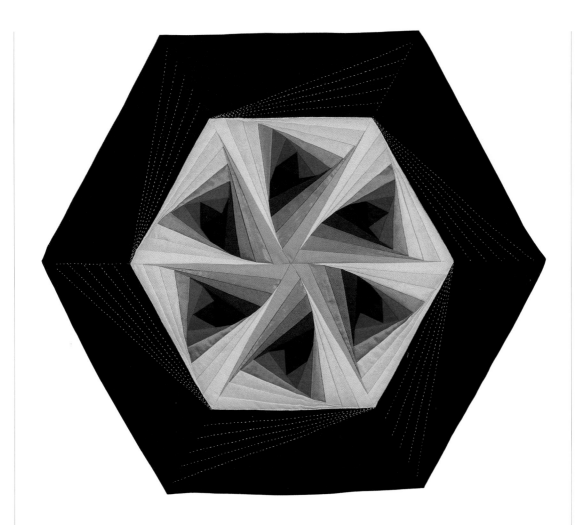

ABOVE
Plate 15. SUMMERTIME,
1993, 22" x 24" (55cm x 60cm).
Bianca Fischer, Dübendorf,
Switzerland.

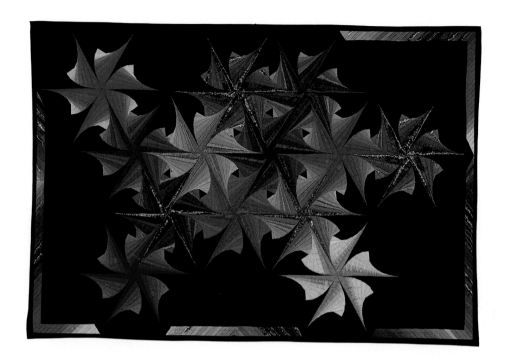

ABOVE
Plate 16. WINDMILLS, 1993,
38" x 54" (95cm x 135cm).
Käthy Gubler, Hirzel, Switzer-
land.

BELOW
Plate 17. WIRBELWIND, 1993,
28" x 20" (70cm x 50cm). Ruth
Keller, Gossau, Switzerland.

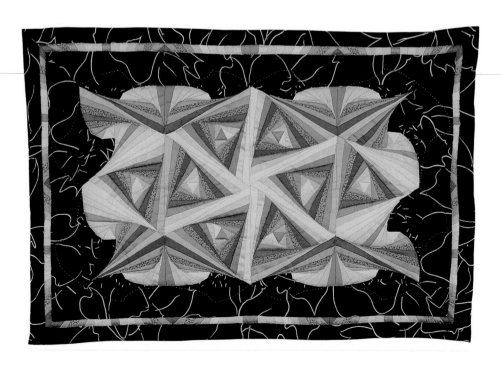

MIRROR IMAGE DESIGNS

The number of design possibilities is greatly increased by combining blocks with clockwise and counterclockwise twist. Blocks with opposite twist are also called mirror images.

To draw a mirror image block follow steps 1 – 6 as described in How to Draw the Pattern on page 36, except instead of measuring in a clockwise direction you now measure in a *counterclockwise* direction. See Figure 43. If you have done everything correctly the result should look exactly like Appendix B5.

For the following steps use copies of Appendix B6 and B3. Cut out three blocks of each of the appendices (three with clockwise, three with counterclockwise twist). Compose a hexagon (as in Step 2 on page 38), alternating blocks with clockwise and counterclockwise twist. See Figure 44.

A new shape emerges across the borders of two adjacent blocks, called the fan. Two sets of three fans each become visible, one set pointing with the narrow ends toward the center of the hexagon, the other set pointing away from the center. See Figure 45.

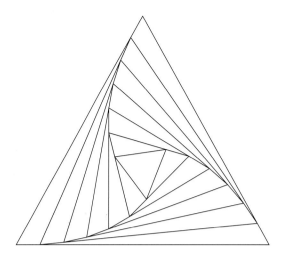

ABOVE
Figure 43. Equilateral triangle in a counterclockwise direction.

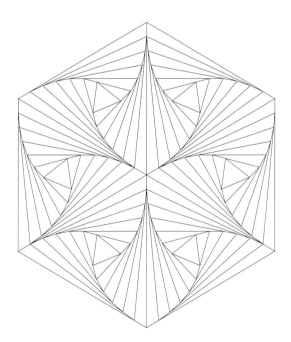

ABOVE
Figure 44. Six equilateral triangles forming a hexagon.

ABOVE
Figure 45. Fans.

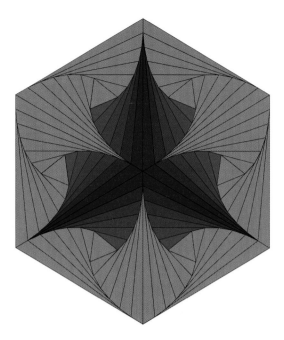

ABOVE
Figure 46. Three fans colored.

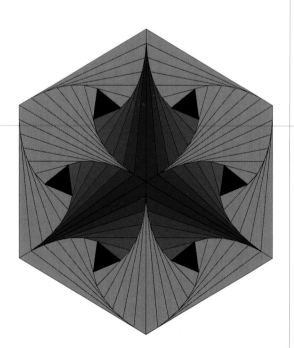

ABOVE
Figure 47. Three fans with center colored.

For the following coloring variations use copies of Appendix B7.

As a first version color the set of three fans pointing with their heads toward the center with six colors of a color range, starting with the two largest strips at the center of each fan (or at the edge of each block if you want to look at it this way).

Color the remainder of the hexagon (including the six centers of the blocks) with the background color. See Figure 46.

Do this version again with the variation of coloring the center of each block with one additional color of your color range, instead of leaving it in the background hue. The resulting design now resembles a fish or a blossom. See Figure 47.

More design combinations are easily achieved by using the colors in reversed order or by using two to three colors alternately.

As an alternate version, color the strips of the fans in one set using one color range, then color the strips of the fans in the other set using a second color range. The centers of the six blocks in the hexagon and the outermost half-fans are blank and should be colored with a background color. See Figure 48.

More striking designs are obtained simply by adding another ring of equilateral triangles around your core hexagon. The result is still a hexagon, although bigger. It takes 12 more equilateral blocks to add one ring. To add yet another ring you need another 24 blocks.

To make your own designs with more blocks you may use copies of Appendix B3 and B6. See Plates 18 through 23, pages 45 through 48.

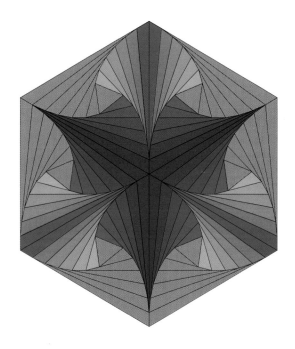

LEFT
Figure 48. Fans colored with two color ranges.

LEFT
Plate 18. VIOLET STAR, 1991, 26" x 26" (65cm x 65cm). Eveline Rufer, Amriswil, Switzerland.

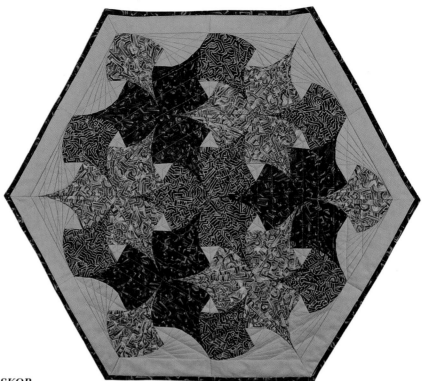

RIGHT
*Plate 19. KALEIDOSKOP
(front), 1991, 24" x 28" (60cm x
70cm). Barbara T. Kaempfer,
Mettmenstetten, Switzerland.*

BELOW RIGHT
*Plate 20. KALEIDOSKOP
(back).*

Plate 21. STAR, 1992, 30" x 26" (75cm x 65cm). Edith Abt, Münchenstein, Switzerland.

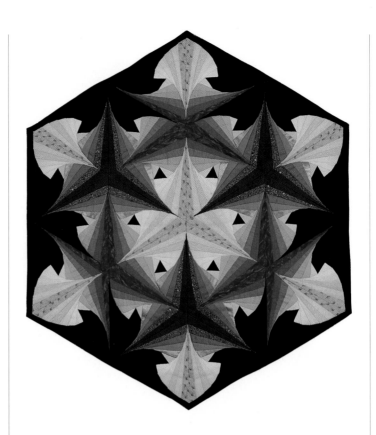

ABOVE
Plate 22. UNTITLED, 1993,
22" x 24" (55cm x 60cm). Klara
Hagen, Murg-Niederdorf,
Germany.

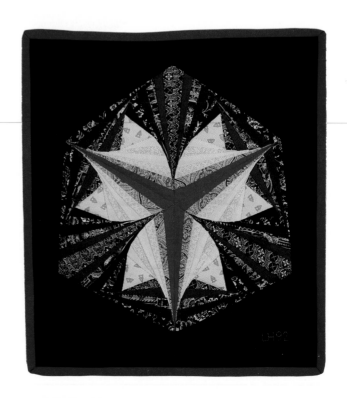

RIGHT
Plate 23. STIEFMÜTTERCHEN
(Pansy), 1992, 18" x 16" (45cm
x 40cm). Lucia Harnischberg,
Bonstetten, Switzerland.

The 90° Triangle

A square diagonally cut in half yields two 90° triangles. Using 90° triangles in a twisted Log Cabin pattern can lead to some striking designs.

The following steps will help you draw and design a twisted Log Cabin pattern based on a right angle triangle.

ABOVE
Plate 24. BLÜTEN (Blossoms), 1993, 28" x 28" (70cm x 70cm). Barbara T. Kaempfer, Mettmenstetten, Switzerland.

49

HOW TO DRAW THE PATTERN

As with all patterns you need a C-Thru™ (see-through) ruler and a pencil or set of colored pencils. Try to work accurately from the start because mistakes can add up quickly.

BLOCK SIZE

All of the examples in this chapter are based on a 6" triangle. I suggest you use this measurement for your first design. If you decide to use a different size you will need to recalculate the measurements.

ADDING TWIST

Again, for your first design efforts I would recommend using the ¾" measurement used in the following example. Note that the shorter this unit of measurement, the greater the twist, and the number of strips required for the design increases.

DRAWING THE PATTERN

Step 1. Use graph paper with preprinted cross sections (preprinted 16 squares per inch, also called 4 sq/in).

Start drawing a square with a 6" side length, but draw only two lines, forming a 90° corner. Draw the diagonal. The resulting shape is a right angle (90°) triangle with two equal sides.

This is called the A-triangle. Mark the corners of the A-triangle A1, A2, and A3 in a clockwise direction. See Figure 49.

Step 2. Starting at corner A1, measure ¾" along the line toward corner A2. Mark this point on the line. Name it B1. Repeat this step in a clockwise direction for the line between A2 and A3. Mark this point and name it B2. Repeat the step again for the line between A3 and A1, resulting in the mark B3. See Figure 50.

Step 3. Connect the B-points with straight lines: B1 with B2, B2 with B3, and B3 with B1. The result is a smaller rotated triangle whose corners touch the lines of your A-triangle. This smaller triangle is called the B-triangle.

If you use a different color pencil for each triangle

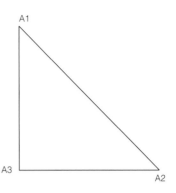

ABOVE
Figure 49. A-triangle.

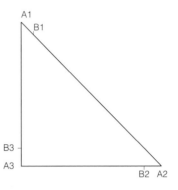

ABOVE
Figure 50. A-triangle with marked B-points.

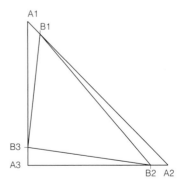

ABOVE
Figure 51. B-triangle inside A-triangle.

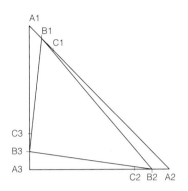

ABOVE

Figure 52. A- and B-triangle with marked C-points.

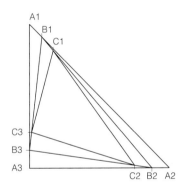

ABOVE

Figure 53. A-, B-, and C-triangle.

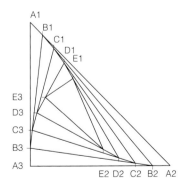

ABOVE

Figure 54. Finished triangle.

it may be easier to verify that you have completed each one. See Figure 51.

Step 4. Now measure and mark ¾" from the B-points along the B-lines in the clockwise direction, producing points C1, C2, and C3. See Figure 52.

Step 5. Connect the C-points to get the C-triangle. The C-triangle is even smaller than the B-triangle, is rotated, and its corners touch the B-triangle. See Figure 53.

Step 6. Repeat steps 4 and 5 until you have four smaller triangles (B to E) in your six inch 90° A-triangle. See Figure 54.

It is important to work in a very precise manner.

If you have done everything correctly, the result of your work should look exactly like appendix C1.

You have now completed the drawing of the basic block with a clockwise twist.

OTHER BLOCK SIZES
AND MEASUREMENTS

The following table shows some useful proportions for blocks of different sizes:

Side length of the block	Unit of measurement for twist
8 inches	1" or ¾"
6 inches	¾" or ½"
4 inches	½" or ¼"
2 inches	¼"

I suggest you try other proportions as well.

COMBINING BLOCKS INTO A DESIGN (ON PAPER)

For almost all designs based on the 90° triangle, you first put together two triangles to form a square, which then becomes the basic building block for larger designs. See Figure 55, page 52.

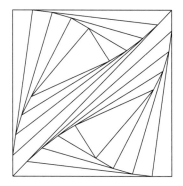

ABOVE
Figure 55. Two 90° triangles form a square.

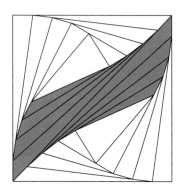

ABOVE
Figure 56. Twisted ribbon.

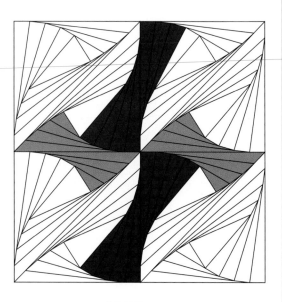

ABOVE
Figure 57. Four-Patch with two ribbons twisted differently.

REDUCING THE DESIGN AND COLORING EFFORT

During the design phase you will do a lot of coloring with colored pencils. Again, using reduced copies of the original 6" design saves both time and effort. To make reductions you can:

- make photocopies on a copier that has a reduction feature
- draw the pattern again with a smaller A-triangle and photocopy it
- make copies of the reduced designs in Appendix C2.

COMBINING BLOCKS

Along the diagonal line where the two diagonals meet, a twisted ribbon becomes visible. See Figure 56.

Step 1. Put together four blocks (cut them out from Appendix C2) to form a Four-Patch with all the diagonal lines running in the same direction. Two new shapes of twisted ribbons emerge along the horizontal and vertical lines of the four blocks. See Figure 57.

This Four-Patch now shows twisted ribbons of three different shapes. See Figure 58.

Step 2. For another variation put four blocks together (cut out from Appendix C2) in such a way that the diagonal lines all run to the center of the Four-Patch.

The four twisted ribbons along the horizontal and vertical lines of the four blocks all have the same uneven shape. See Figure 59.

Step 3. Emphasize the twisted ribbons by coloring; use copies of Appendix C3 (a Four-Patch) for the following steps.

As with the equilateral triangle, it is easier to start coloring an assembled Four- or Nine-Patch instead of coloring an individual block. You can see all the block-crossing twisted ribbons before you start coloring them.

a. Choose three color ranges, each of four colors (or shades) plus one background color (a total of 13 colors). For this example I suggest you choose four different shades (or hues) of each of green, yellow, and brown, plus black for the background.

b. First let's color one strip with one shade of brown along the diagonal line of the top left block. Select another strip at random in the other half of this ribbon and color it with exactly the same shade of brown. The only choice to be avoided in this coloring pattern is to color the two longest strips (the strips that meet at the diagonal lines) with the same shade.

c. Next use the same shade of brown (the one you used in step 3b) to color the two strips of the same ribbons of the next block. It doesn't matter which two strips you choose, as long as you select one in each half of the twisted ribbon. In fact, this design looks more interesting if you use the same shade of a color on different strips of the same ribbons in other blocks. Continue coloring two strips in the same ribbons in each of the remaining blocks with this same shade of brown.

When you have completed this step, your Nine-Patch will have a total of 18 strips colored with the same shade of brown. See Figure 60, page 54.

d. Select another shade of brown. Color two strips in each of the same twisted ribbons at random (one strip per half ribbon).

As a result, in some ribbons two adjacent strips will now be colored in two different shades; in others there are still gaps between the colored strips. The more variations you try, the better. See Figure 61, page 54.

e. Repeat step 3d two more times, using the remaining two shades of brown. See Figure 62, page 55.

f. Repeat steps 3b – 3e for the twisted ribbons where the horizontal lines of the blocks meet using the four shades of green you selected in step 3a.

g. Repeat steps 3b – 3e for the twisted ribbons where the vertical lines of the blocks meet using the four shades of yellow you selected in step 3a.

h. Color the remaining space – the half ribbons along the outer edge of the Nine-Patch and the center of each 90° triangle – with the background color (in this example, black). The end result of your labor should look like Figure 63, page 55.

Step 4. If you join the blocks as shown in step 2 and use different color ranges (in this example brown, yellow, and green) another design results. However,

ABOVE
Figure 58. Four-Patch with
three different twisted ribbons.

ABOVE
Figure 59. Four-Patch with
diagonals toward the center.

RIGHT
Figure 60. Eighteen strips colored with one shade of brown.

RIGHT
Figure 61. Eighteen more strips colored with a second shade of brown.

LEFT
Figure 62. Brown ribbons colored.

BELOW
Figure 63. Nine-Patch colored.

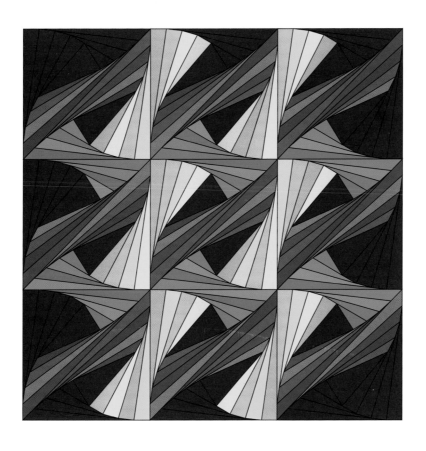

ABOVE
Figure 64. Four-Patch colored.

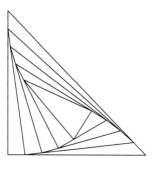

ABOVE
Figure 65. 90° triangle in counterclockwise direction.

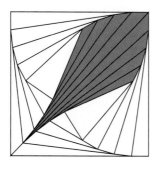

ABOVE
Figure 66. Two 90° triangles form a fan.

the coloring technique is the same.

Appendix C4 is provided for your convenience to create your own design just by selecting a variety of colors. See Figure 64.

MIRROR IMAGE DESIGNS

As with the forms described in Chapter 1 and 2, the number of designs is dramatically increased by combining blocks with a clockwise and counterclockwise twist. Blocks with twists turning in opposite directions are also known as mirror images.

To draw a mirror image block follow steps 1 – 6 as described in Drawing the Pattern on pages 50 – 51, except instead of measuring in a clockwise direction, now measure in a counterclockwise direction. See Figure 65.

The result of your drawing should look exactly like Appendix C5.

As already mentioned in Combining Blocks into a Design (on Paper) on page 52, two 90° triangles are joined to form a square which then becomes the basic building block for larger designs. This time one 90° triangle has a clockwise twist, the other a counterclockwise twist. The emerging shape along the diagonal line is a fan. For the following color and design steps use copies of Appendix C6. See Figure 66.

Step 1. Join four blocks (cut out from Appendix C6) to form a Four-Patch with all diagonal lines running in the same direction.

Four identical fans of an uneven shape become visible where the horizontal and vertical lines of the four blocks meet. In this assembly of the Four-Patch two types of fans are visible. See Figure 67.

Step 2. Assembling the four blocks with the heads of the fan along the diagonal with all fans pointing toward the center of the Four-Patch results in the pattern shown in Figure 68.

Step 3. Another variation is created by joining the four blocks with the tails of the fans along the diagonal all pointing toward the center of the Four-Patch. See Figure 69.

Step 4. Emphasize the fans by coloring; use copies of Appendix C7 (a Nine-Patch) for the following steps.

Steps 4a – 4h. Follow steps 3a – 3h on page 52 through 56 but this time color the fans instead of the twisted ribbons. The result of your efforts should look like Figure 71, page 58.

Step 5. Next, let's color the pattern created in step 2 of this chapter. Use copies of Appendix C8 for the following design steps.

You may use different color ranges; the coloring technique is the same as described previously.

Figure 70 (page 58) shows what may result (depending on the color choice).

Step 6. Next, let's color the pattern created in step 3 of this chapter. Use copies of Appendix C9 for the following design steps. Figure 72, page 59 might be the result.

Composing several Four- or Nine-Patches (like you just created) into larger designs could result in a beautiful quilt. See Plates 25 through 29, pages 59 through 63.

ABOVE
Figure 67. Four-Patch with two different fans.

BELOW LEFT
Figure 68. Four-Patch with heads of fans pointing toward the center.

BELOW
Figure 69. Four-Patch with tails of fan pointing toward center.

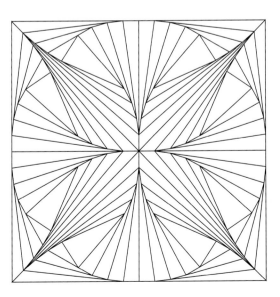

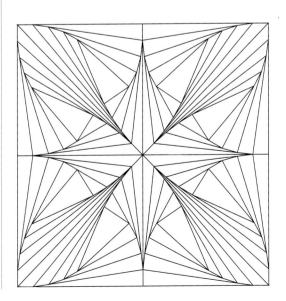

RIGHT
Figure 70. Four-Patch with heads of colored fans pointing to the center.

BELOW
Figure 71. Nine-Patch of colored fans.

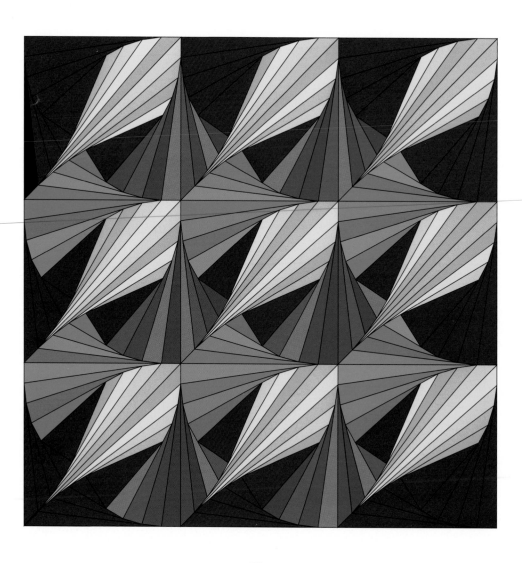

Figure 72. Four-Patch with tails of colored fans pointing to center of the block.

BELOW
Plate 25. HERBSTBLÄTTER (Autumn Leaves), 1992, 32″ x 32″ (80cm x 80cm). Silvia Achermann, Hirzel, Switzerland.

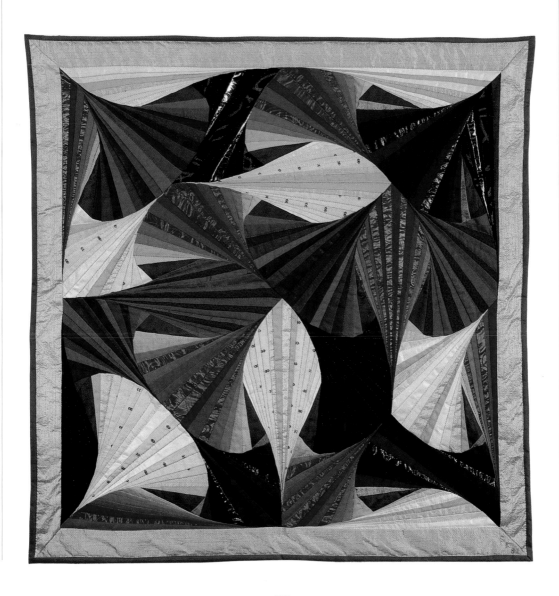

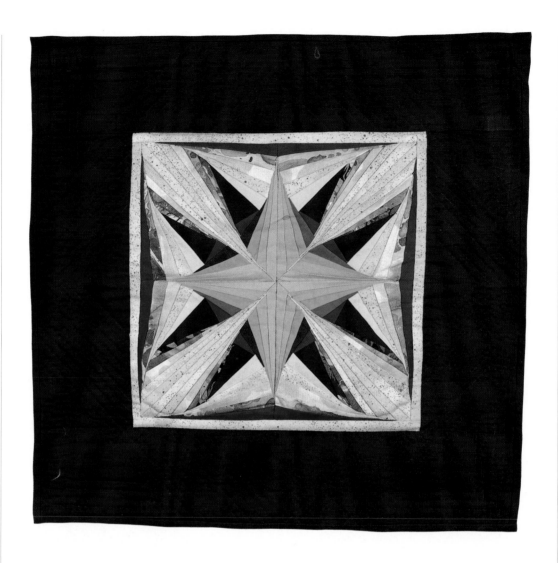

**Plate 26. SUNSHINE, 1993,
22" x 22" (55cm x 55cm). Lotti
Fuss, Safenwil, Switzerland.**

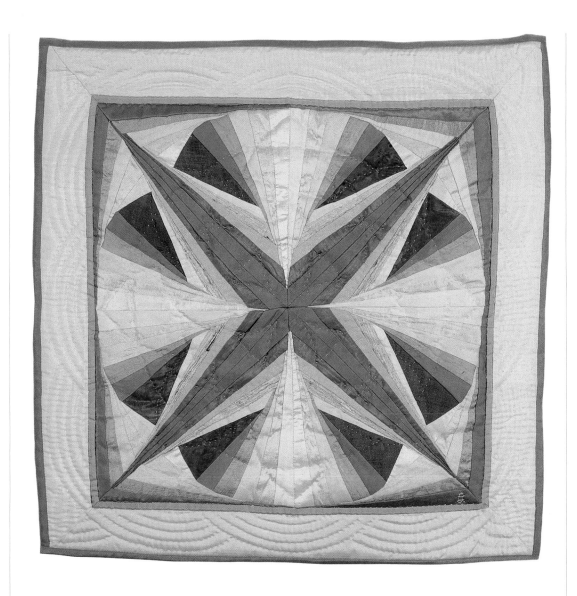

**Plate 27. SHOOTING STAR,
1994, 20" x 20" (50cm x 50cm).
Lotti Fuss, Safenwil, Switzerland.**

ABOVE
Plate 28. ROTE ERDE (Red Soil) 1993, 54" x 54" (135 cm x 135cm). Erika Ghidossi, Schaffhausen, Switzerland.

ABOVE
Plate 29. UNTITLED, 1994,
16" x 16" (40cm x 40cm). Ruth
Fux, Zermatt, Switzerland.

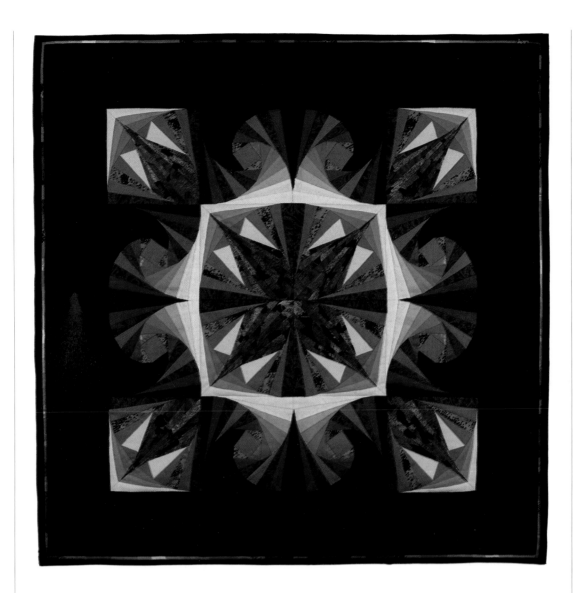

Combinations and Other Shapes

This chapter shows you some combinations of blocks you learned to create in previous chapters. In addition, other forms like diamonds and hexagons are discussed.

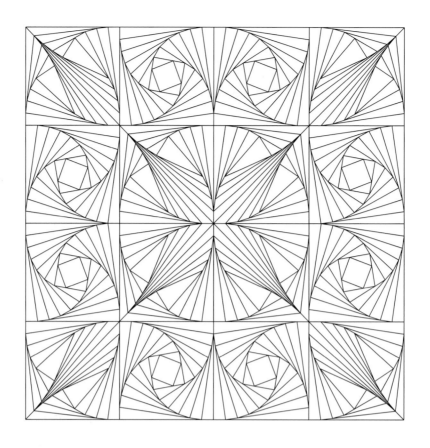

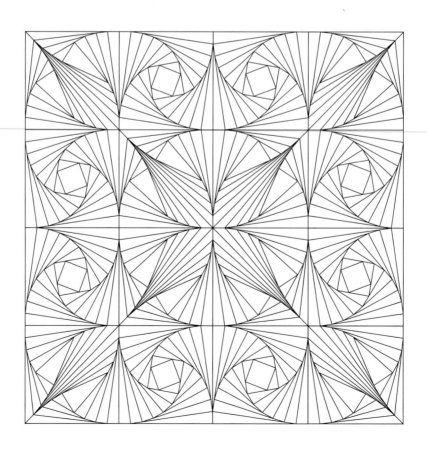

COMBINING SQUARES AND RIGHT ANGLE TRIANGLES

This is where the real fun starts!

If you want to compose a quilt from blocks of different shapes, the individual blocks need to have the same side length. The quilt shown on page 65 is made entirely of squares and right-angle triangles, as described in Chapters 1 and 3. By using four blocks from appendix A2, four blocks from Appendix A5, and eight blocks from Appendix C6 you can create this pattern. See Figure 73, top of page 66.

The quilt below is made entirely of just two blocks of Appendix C6 and two blocks of Appendix A5.

I encourage you to try creating your own combinations. See Plate 31 and Plate 32, page 69.

OPPOSITE TOP
Figure 73. Design using squares and triangles by Lydia Fux.

OPPOSITE BOTTOM
Figure 74. This is another design using squares and triangles by Lydia Fux.

BELOW
Plate 31. BARBARA, 1993, 20" x 20" (50cm x 50cm). Lilian Marquis, Münchenstein, Switzerland.

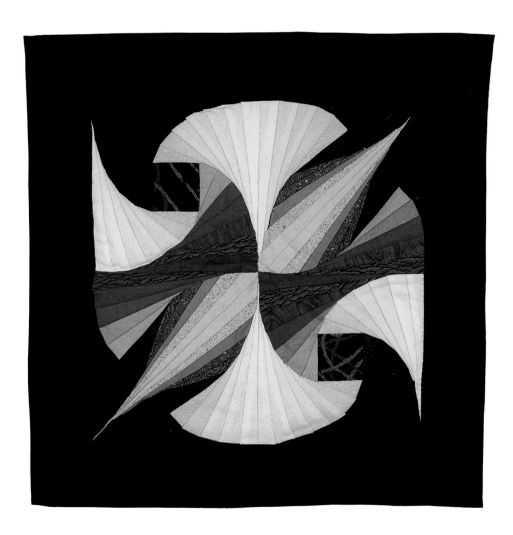

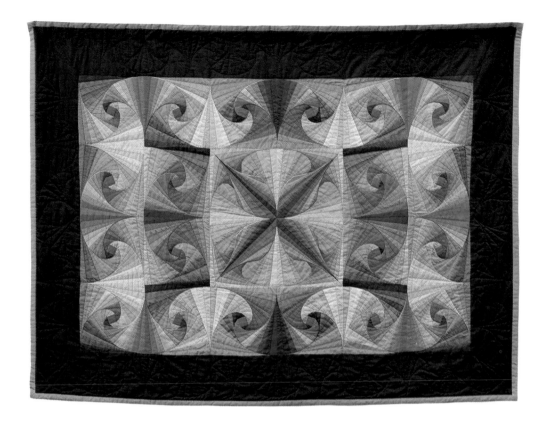

OPPOSITE TOP LEFT
Figure 75. Another design variation using squares and triangles.

OPPOSITE BOTTOM LEFT
Figure 76. A second design variation using squares and triangles.

ABOVE
**Plate 32. DANI'S QUILT, 1993,
60" x 84" (150cm x 210cm).
Rita Schmid, Obfelden,
Switzerland.**

COMBINING EQUILATERAL TRIANGLES
WITH DIAMONDS

OPPOSITE TOP
Figure 77. Uncolored design by Doris Beyeler.

OPPOSITE BOTTOM
Figure 78. Diamonds and equilaterals.

BELOW
Plate 33. FANTASY IN BLUE, 1993, 34" x 30" (85cm x 75cm). Doris Beyeler, Ramsen, Switzerland.

If you'd like to combine equilateral triangle blocks with some other shape, I recommend you start with the diamond. To draw a diamond follow the directions in Chapter 2. Use copies of Appendix B1 and draw a diamond instead of an equilateral triangle. Otherwise the drawing steps are the same. Construct a diamond with the same side length as the equilateral triangle. See the examples on pages 71 through 74.

The quilt below, Plate 33, is made of:
- six blocks of equilateral triangles (clockwise, Appendix B3)
- six blocks of equilateral triangles (counterclockwise, Appendix B6)
- three blocks of diamonds (clockwise, Appendix D1)
- three blocks of diamonds (counterclockwise, Appendix D2).

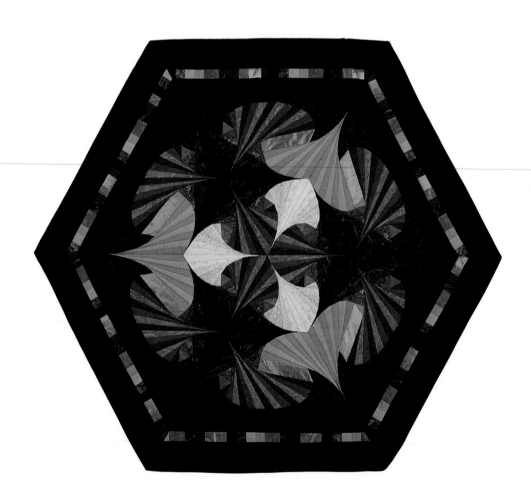

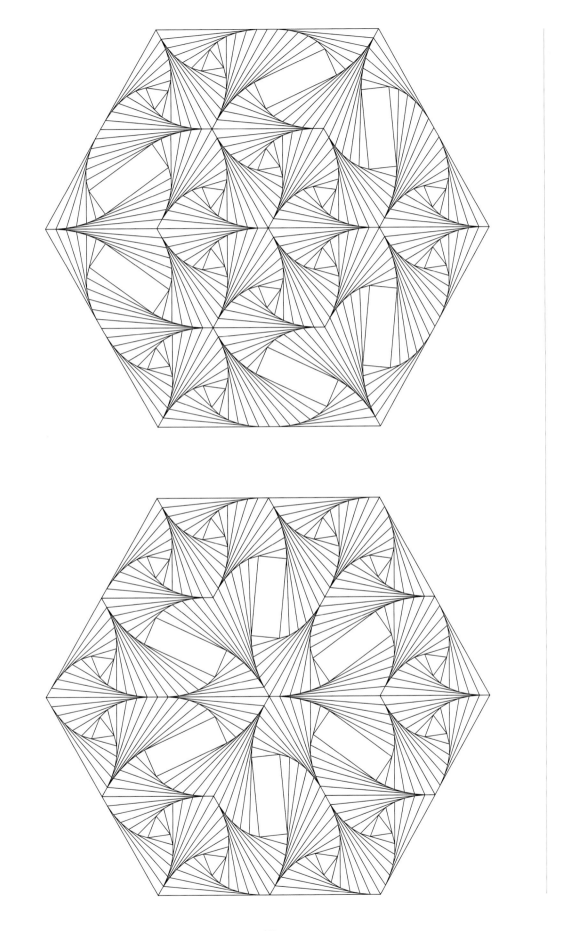

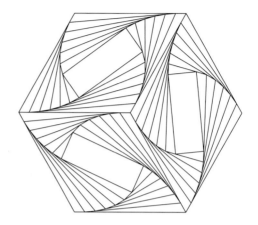

TOP AND BELOW
Figures 79 and 80. Other samples using diamonds.

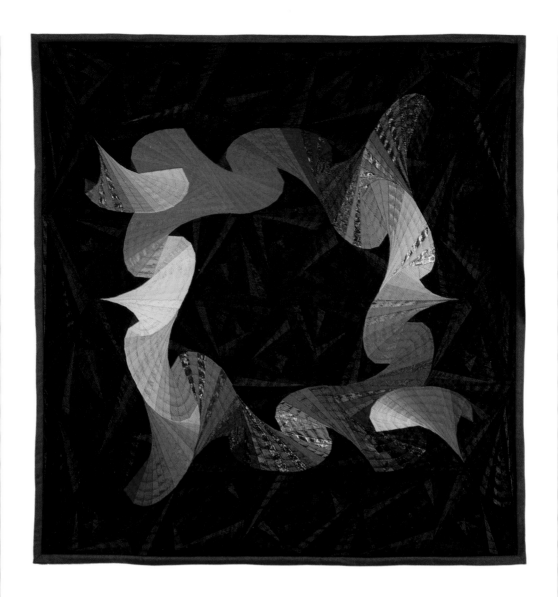

ABOVE
Plate 34. WAVES, 1993, 40" x 41" (100cm x 104cm). Käthy Gubler, Hirzel, Switzerland.

Plate 35. ORANGE BLOSSOM SPECIAL, 1994, 36" x 32" (90cm x 80cm). Aranka Nemeth-Hopp, St. Gallen, Switzerland.

THE HEXAGON

Another basic shape for a block is the hexagon.

To draw a hexagon follow the directions in Chapter 2. Use copies of Appendix B1 and draw a hexagon as the A-figure instead of an equilateral triangle. Otherwise the drawing steps are the same. Use copies of Appendix D3 and D4 to create your own designs. The following two quilts are made up entirely of hexagons. See Plates 36 and 37, pages 75 and 76.

OTHER COMBINATIONS

Other combinations of shapes that may lead to very interesting designs are:
- the equilateral triangle and the hexagon
- the hexagon and the diamond
- the hexagon, the equilateral, and the diamond
- square and equilateral
- square and diamond.

A basic rule to be observed is that all the blocks to be combined in one design *must* have the same side length.

BELOW
Plate 36. OHNE TITEL, 1993, 24" x 28" (60cm x 70cm). Gisela Pugni-Spatz, Freiburg i. Breisgau, Germany.

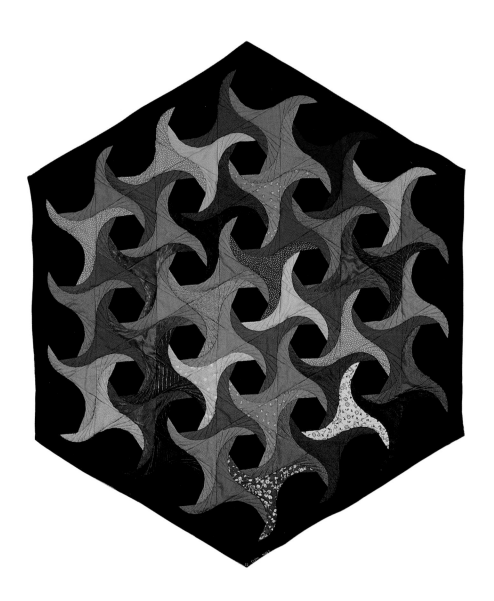

ABOVE
Plate 37. VENTO VERSATA,
1991, 38" x 40" (95cm x
100cm). Barbara T. Kaempfer,
Mettmenstetten, Switzerland.

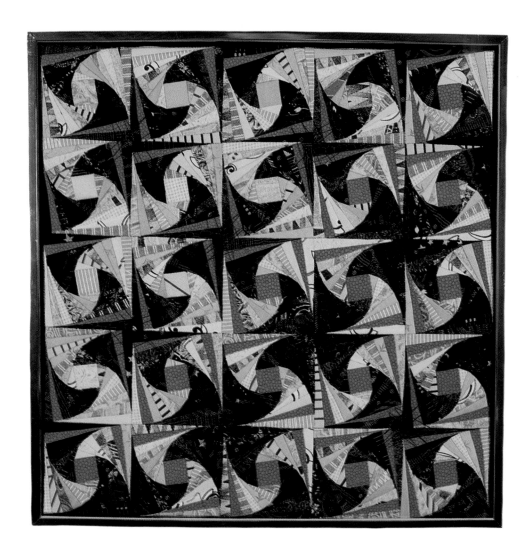

Sewing and Finishing the Quilt

This chapter describes how to prepare a foundation, how to choose the quality and colors of the fabric, how to sew the block, how to put the quilt together, and gives some hints about the quilting.

PREPARING THE FOUNDATION

The blocks are sewn on a foundation, which can be made from several different materials. Regardless of which material you use, it is very important that the marking lines of your foundations are drawn accurately. These marking lines will be your sewing lines.

Before starting to draw your blocks on the foundation, you have to keep in mind that you will be sewing on the wrong side (the backside) of the block. This means if the blocks in your design appear only with a clockwise twist (for example, twisted ribbon) the foundations you'll need must all show a counterclockwise twist.

Add ½" seam allowance on all sides of the foundations.

MATERIALS FOR THE FOUNDATION

Paper: You may use almost any lightweight paper. I recommend you make copies of the original drawing of a block to be used as foundations. Always keep the originals safe! If you work with a pattern shown in this book, the foundation worksheets in the Appendices may serve as originals. Make copies on a high quality copying machine in order to avoid distortions. Verify with a ruler that the measurements on the copies are the same as on the original.

Fabric: If you use fabric as a foundation you may:
- Cut the whole foundation block from fabric you are using for the center piece of the block. This results in a single layered center piece.
- Use a neutral fabric. This result is a double-layered center piece. I recommend preshrunk cotton.

Don't forget to add ½" seam allowance on all sides.

To mark the fabric use a light box or mark it with tracing paper used by professional dressmakers.

Other methods: Other methods for foundation piecing are well described in the book *Precision Pieced Quilts Using the Foundation Method* by Jane Hall and Dixie Haywood.

Mark the colors of each strip on the foundation.

ABOVE
Figure 81. Strips of fabric in shades of one color.

BELOW
Figure 82. Strips of fabric in adjacent colors on the color wheel.

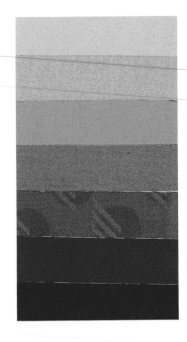

Since the pattern is drawn in mirror image on the sewing side of the foundation, it is easy to confuse the colors during sewing. To avoid this mishap, I recommend you mark the color of the fabric on the sewing side of the foundation.

Once you have prepared all your foundations you are ready to select the fabric and start sewing.

ABOVE
Figure 83. Strips of solid colors in the same hue.

BELOW
Figure 84. Printed fabrics of the same hue.

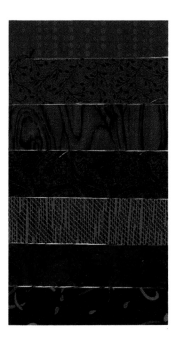

CHOOSING AND CUTTING THE FABRIC

QUALITY OF FABRIC

For the first quilt you make using this technique I recommend you use only lightweight cotton. It is easier to handle than other types of fabric such as silk. I always preshrink all the fabrics. Once you have some experience with this technique you might want to use other types of fabrics (silk, blends, etc.) which give very pretty results. The most difficult fabrics to work with are those with a very thick texture such as woolens.

COLOR RANGES

The term "color range" as used in this book may have several interchangeable meanings:
- Shades of one color (light to dark blue). See Figure 81, page 78.
- Subsequent colors in the color wheel (yellow – orange – red). See Figure 82, page 78.
- Different fabrics with the same color hue (very nice for backgrounds). See Figures 83 and 84.

CHOOSING THE FABRIC

Refer to your colored design on paper (in reduced scale) to determine how many different fabrics you need.

ESTIMATING THE QUANTITY OF FABRIC NEEDED

It is impossible to give reliable directions on how to calculate the quantity of each fabric needed, because it depends on so many factors:

- the design you chose or created
- the colors chosen
- the shapes.

Just use common sense, and if in doubt, buy more for your first quilt. You will quickly gain experience in estimating the quantities needed as you make more quilts.

I always cut only one strip from each color for my first block and sew it. When I'm pleased with the result and am sure that I selected the right colors, I cut more strips.

For a smaller quilt project (like SONJA, page 11) I used a fat quarter per color, border not included.

CUTTING THE FABRIC

Cut the fabric into strips. The width of the strip is determined by the distance between the A and B points of your foundation plus seam allowance. For instance, if the distance between A and B points is ¾", add ½" (2 x ¼") seam allowance, resulting in 1¼" wide strips.

Always cut your strips from selvage to selvage. As usual in quilting, never use the selvage itself, cut if off.

Don't cut the strips into pieces now.

Determine the size of the center piece. Add ¼" seam allowance on each side. Cut it.

SEWING THE BLOCK

GET YOURSELF ORGANIZED

- Make sure your sewing machine is in good working condition.
- Select one of the smaller stitches (about 18 per inch).
- Select a thread that does not contrast too much with most of the colors of your project. (I often use gray.)
- Arrange the strips of fabric on one side of your working area in the order you will be using them (from the center toward the edge of the block).

RIGHT
Plate 39. LIGHT AND DARK WITH A TWIST, 1994, 24" x 24" (60cm x 60cm). Barbara T. Kaempfer, Mettmenstetten, Switzerland.

- Turn your iron on and place it within reach. The iron does not need to be a steam iron, but if you use one, iron on the fabric side of your block only, because the steam will adversely affect your paper foundation.
- Place the colored design of your quilt project in a place where you can see it all the time.

Now you are all set to get started!

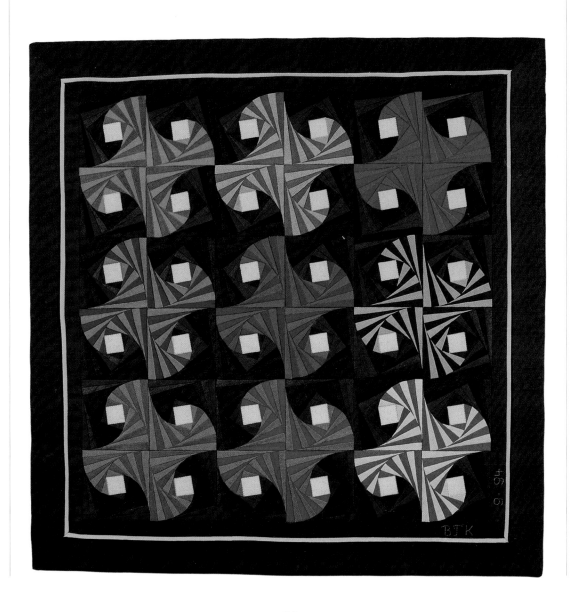

ABOVE
Figure 85. Unmarked side of foundation with center piece.

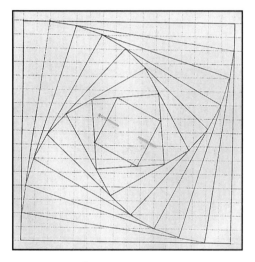

ABOVE
Figure 86. Marked side of foundation with center piece not visible.

ABOVE
Figure 87. Unmarked side of foundation with first strip.

SEWING THE BLOCK

Remember that the markings on your foundation are in mirror image on the wrong side. This marked side will face upwards while sewing. The fabric is underneath the paper and you cannot see it. You'll get used to this soon.

Step 1. Place the fabric for your center piece right side down underneath your foundation block (the unmarked side of the foundation and the wrong side of the fabric are touching). Hold the two against the light and adjust the fabric until all the sewing lines are equally covered by the fabric.

Fix the center piece in place with a pin. Always pin from the marked foundation side. See Figures 85 and 86.

Step 2. Place the fabric for the first strip (one of the smallest triangles next to the center) along the sewing line of the center piece (right sides of fabric facing each other).

Pin in place. Do not cut the strip before sewing. See Figures 87 and 88.

Step 3. Sew from corner to corner (on the marked side). See Figure 89, page 83.

Never sew longer than the marked lines. *Don't use backstitches.*

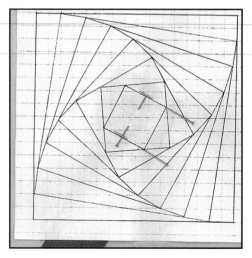

ABOVE
Figure 88. Marked side of foundation with first strip pinned in place.

Step 4. Cut the loose ends of the threads leaving about ¼".

Step 5. Cut the loose end of the strip. See Figure 90.

Step 6. Trim the seam allowance to about ⅛". Finger press and iron (on the fabric side). It is very important to iron every sewn seam. See Figure 91.

Step 7. Repeat steps 2 – 6 for the other three strips on this first square. See Figure 92.

Step 8. Repeat steps 2 – 7 for each round until you have completed the block. Always trim the seam allowance before ironing. See Figure 93, page 84.

Step 9. Trim the excess fabric around the A-square, leaving at least ⅜" seam allowance. Leave the seam allowance on the foundation. See Figure 94, page 84.

Note for steps 2 – 7 for blocks of another shape. If you are working with a shape such as an equilateral triangle, when you add a new strip (or before you trim one you've just sewn), be sure the strip is long enough to cover the entire length of the sewing line of the next strip to be added. See Figure 95, page 84.

ABOVE
Figure 90. Trimmed strip.

ABOVE
Figure 91. Trimmed seam allowance.

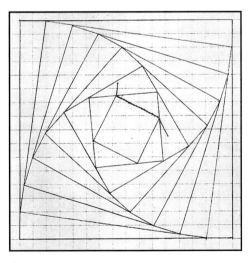

ABOVE
Figure 89. First sewn strip, marked side.

ABOVE
Figure 92. First round sewn.

RIGHT
Figure 93. Completed block.

BELOW RIGHT
Figure 94. Cut the block square.

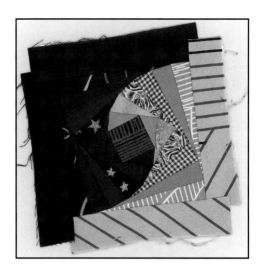

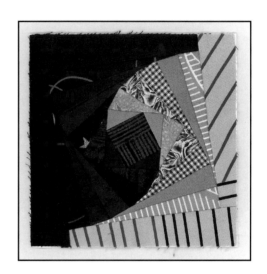

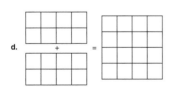

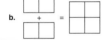

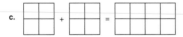

ABOVE
*Figure 96. How to sew the
blocks together. Steps a – d.*

RIGHT
*Figure 95. Equilateral triangle
with first strip sewn.*

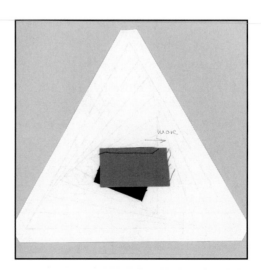

SEWING THE BLOCKS TOGETHER

Once you have completed all the blocks of your quilt you're ready to sew them together.

In my experience it is better to sew blocks together only after you have finished them all, because this way it is simpler to correct any errors. It also provides an opportunity to make any changes to the design at the last minute.

The easiest way to sew your blocks together is by sections, first making pairs, then Four-Patches, and so on. See Figure 96.

The blocks are sewn together along the lines of the A-square on the foundation.

Join the blocks by placing pins at each end of the sewing line first, then add more pins along the line. Work very precisely. See Figure 97.

Sew from raw edge to raw edge. See Figure 98.

Press the seam allowance open. Continue until all your blocks are sewn together into a quilt top.

Note: Add borders *before* removing the paper foundation!

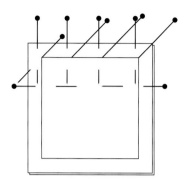

ABOVE
Figure 97. Two blocks pinned together.

REMOVING THE PAPER FOUNDATION

If you plan to have your quilt framed you can leave the paper foundation in your quilt because the stiffness of the paper-layer of the quilt will not matter. It also saves you a lot of work.

To remove the paper foundation, install yourself in a comfortable chair with a pin or tweezers, a waste basket, and a good lamp close by and take your time. Start removing the foundation at one corner of your quilt by gently pulling along a sewing line. As soon as you can grab a paper strip with your fingers, tear it off. Don't pull too hard on the fabric; usually you don't have much seam allowance, so you have to work very carefully! Use a pin or tweezers when needed. Remove the paper foundation strip by strip from the whole quilt.

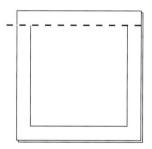

ABOVE
Figure 98. Two blocks sewn together.

QUILTING

THE SANDWICH

You may use any type of batting. I prefer cotton batting because it works best for me with machine quilting. It is very important to baste every block very carefully.

QUILTING

In my opinion the twisted Log Cabin pattern does not require much quilting, especially if you frame it.

Hand Quilting

Since the quilt has many seams, it is difficult to quilt it by hand. If you prefer to quilt by hand, try to quilt along the edges of the strips of the twisted Log Cabin pattern or simply quilt just the center piece. If you have added borders to your project, you may hand quilt those. See Figure 99.

Machine Quilting

I quilt all my twisted Log Cabin projects by machine. You may get very nice effects by emphasizing the twisted lines of your design. The effect may be enhanced by choosing a contrasting thread.

Congratulations, you've just completed a unique quilt! Don't forget to sign it and add the date.

TOP RIGHT
Figure 99. Samples for hand quilting.

BOTTOM RIGHT
Figure 100. Samples for machine quilting.

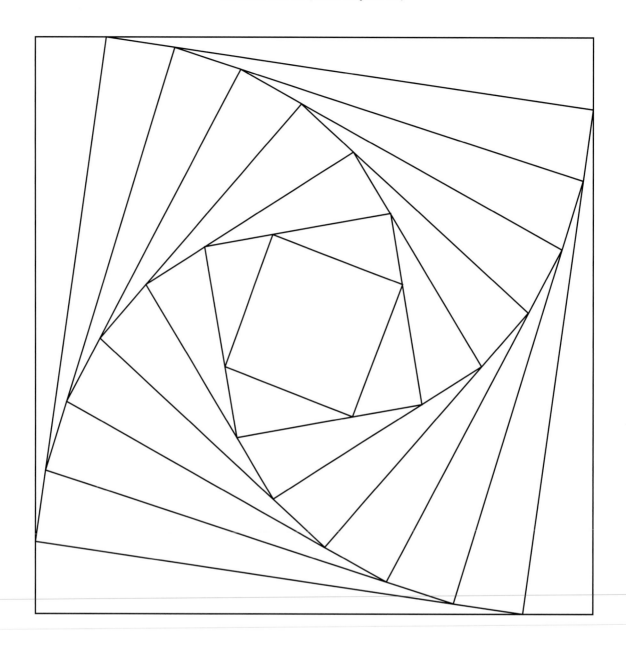

Appendix A
The Square

ABOVE
*Square with 6" side length, ¾"
clockwise twist.*

A1 FOUNDATION WORKSHEET

A2 DESIGN AND COLORING WORKSHEET

ABOVE
*Reduced blocks of squares with
a clockwise twist.*

ABOVE
Joined, reduced blocks of squares with a clockwise twist.

A3 COLORING WORKSHEET

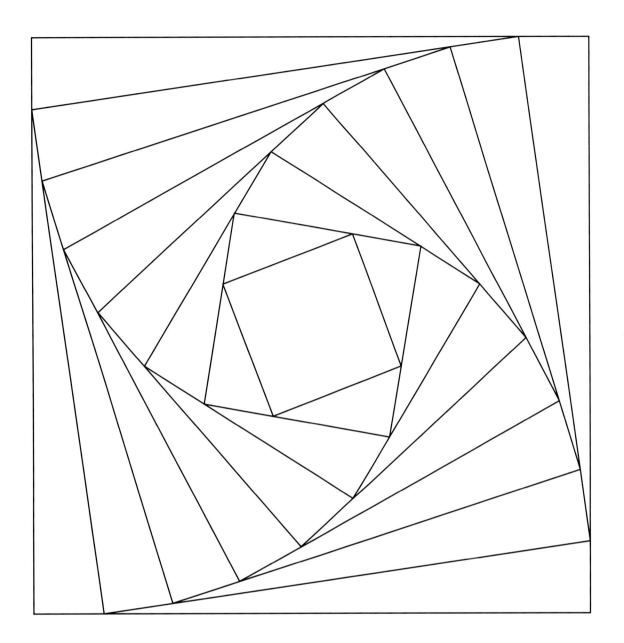

A4 FOUNDATION WORKSHEET

ABOVE
*Square with 6" side length, ¾"
counterclockwise twist.*

ABOVE
Reduced blocks of squares with a counterclockwise twist.

A5 DESIGN AND COLORING WORKSHEET

A6 COLORING WORKSHEET

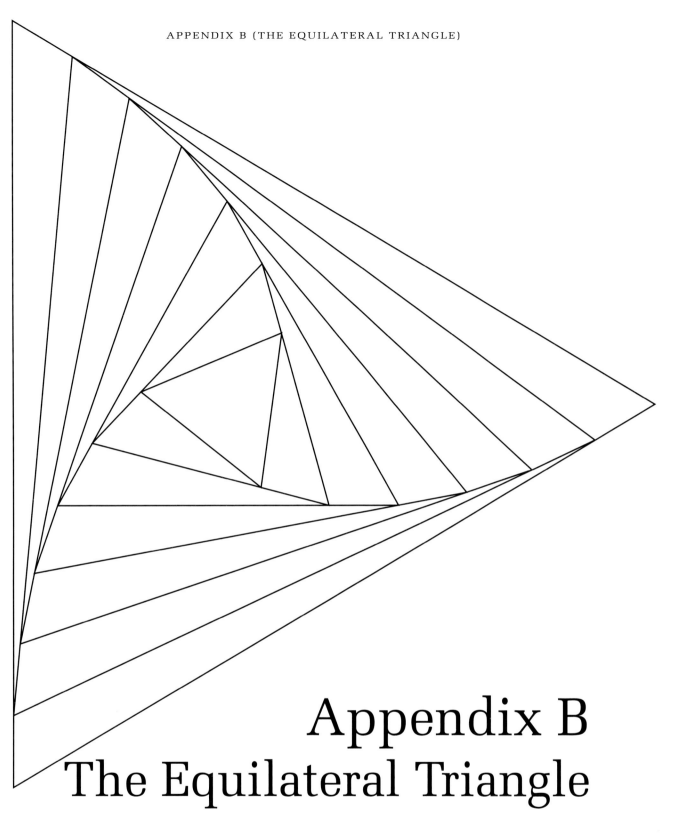

Appendix B
The Equilateral Triangle

B1 DRAWING WORKSHEET, left

B2 FOUNDATION WORKSHEET

LEFT
Isometric page with equilateral triangles.

ABOVE
Equilateral triangles with 8″ side length, ¾″ clockwise twist.

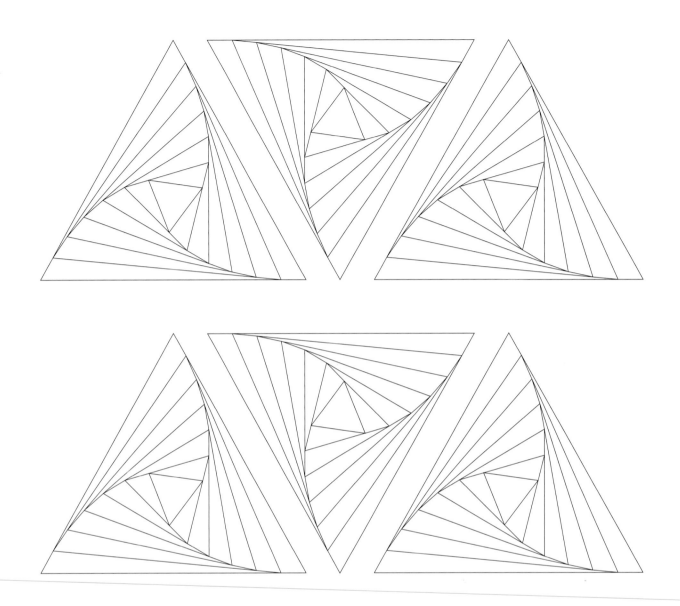

ABOVE
Reduced blocks of equilateral triangles with a clockwise twist.

B3 DESIGN AND COLORING WORKSHEET

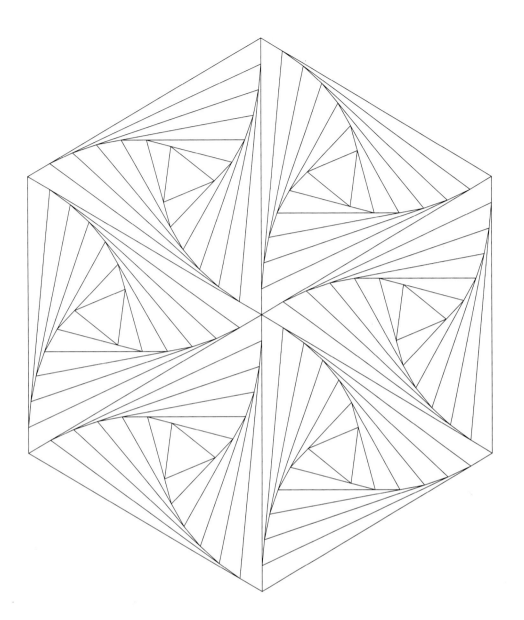

B4 COLORING WORKSHEET

ABOVE
*Hexagon made of six reduced
blocks of equilateral triangles
with a clockwise twist.*

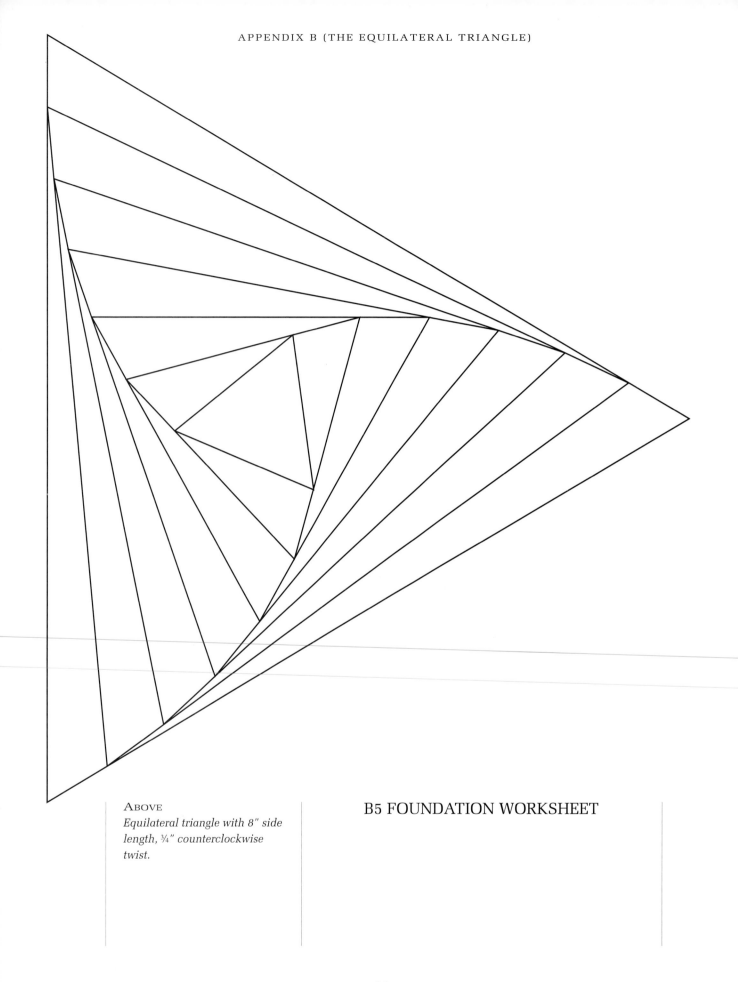

ABOVE
*Equilateral triangle with 8" side
length, ¾" counterclockwise
twist.*

B5 FOUNDATION WORKSHEET

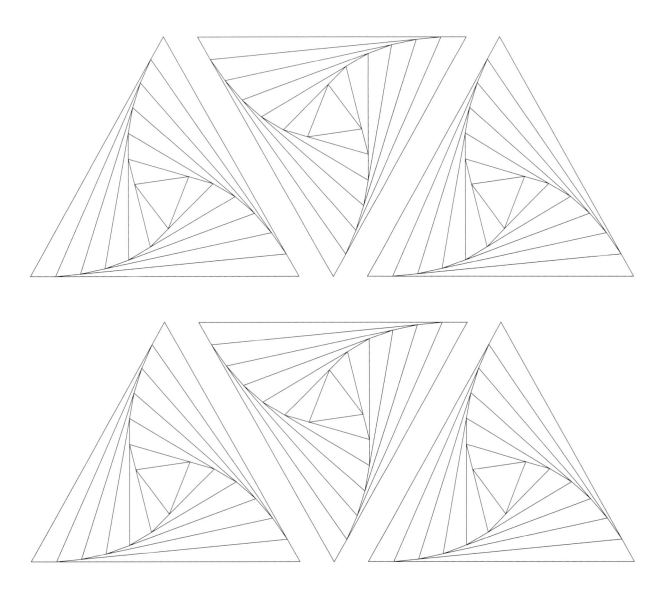

B6 DESIGN AND COLORING WORKSHEET

ABOVE
*Reduced blocks of equilateral
triangles with a counterclockwise twist.*

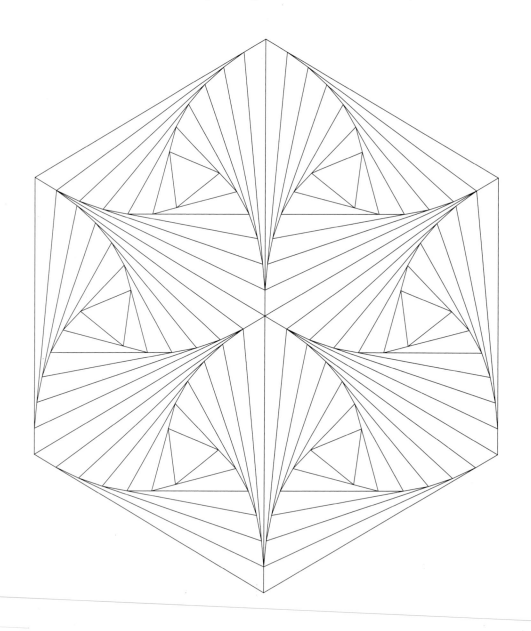

Hexagon made of six reduced blocks of equilateral triangles, clockwise alternating with a counterclockwise twist.

B7 COLORING WORKSHEET

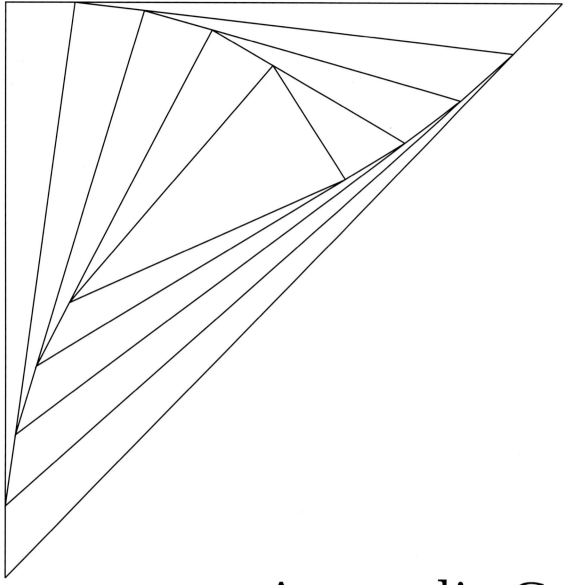

Appendix C
The 90° Triangle

C1 FOUNDATION WORKSHEET

*90° triangle with 6" side length,
¾" clockwise twist.*

101

ABOVE
*Reduced blocks of pairs of 90°
triangles with a clockwise twist,
joined into squares.*

C2 DESIGN AND COLORING WORKSHEET

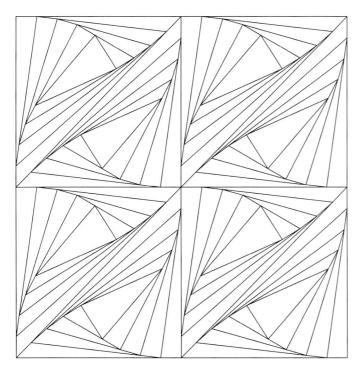

LEFT
Joined reduced blocks of 90° tri-angles with a clockwise twist, diagonals running parallel.

C3 – C4 COLORING WORKSHEETS

ABOVE
Reduced Four-Patch of 90° tri-angles with a clockwise twist, diagonals running to the center.

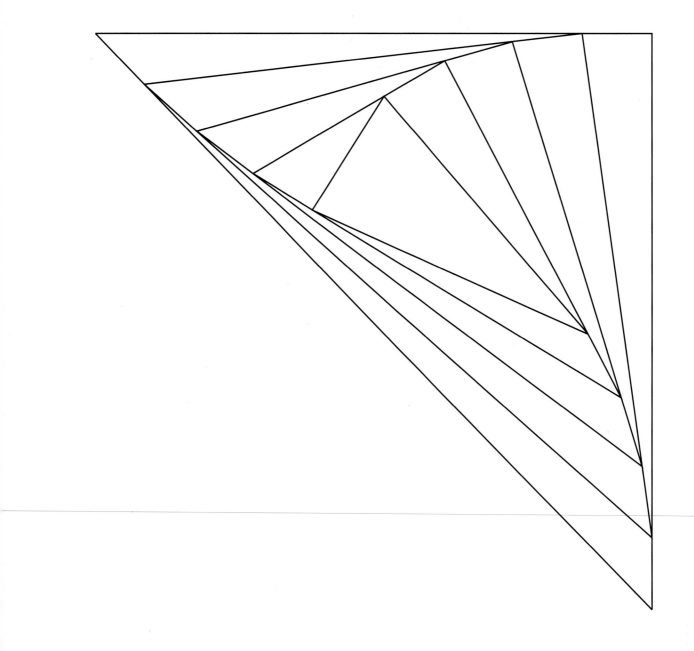

ABOVE

90° triangle with 6" side length, ¾" twist counterclockwise.

C5 FOUNDATION WORKSHEET

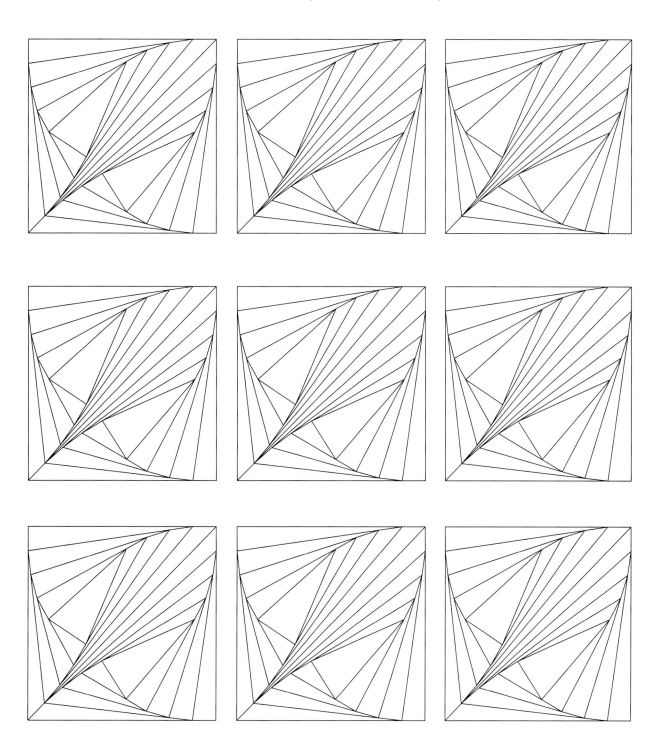

C6 DESIGN AND COLORING WORKSHEET

ABOVE
*Reduced blocks of pairs of 90°
triangles, each pair with a
clockwise and a counterclockwise twist.*

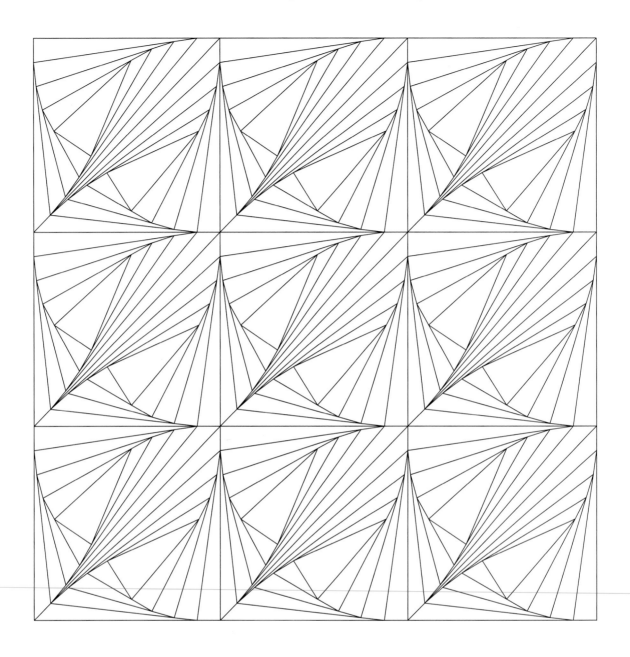

ABOVE
Joined reduced blocks of 90°
triangles, clockwise alternating
with counterclockwise twist,
diagonals running in parallel.

C7 COLORING WORKSHEET

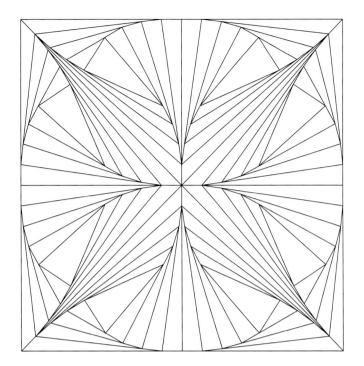

Reduced Four-Patch of pairs of 90° triangles, clockwise alternating with counterclockwise twist, heads of diagonal fans pointing to the center.

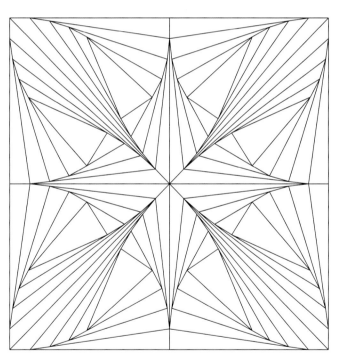

C8 – C9 COLORING WORKSHEETS

Above
Reduced Four-Patch of pairs of 90° triangles, clockwise alternating with counterclockwise twist, tails of diagonal fans pointing to the center.

Appendix D
Diamonds & Hexagons

ABOVE
Reduced blocks of diamonds
with a clockwise twist.

D1 DESIGN AND COLORING WORKSHEET

D2 DESIGN AND COLORING WORKSHEET

ABOVE
*Reduced blocks of diamonds
with a counterclockwise twist.*

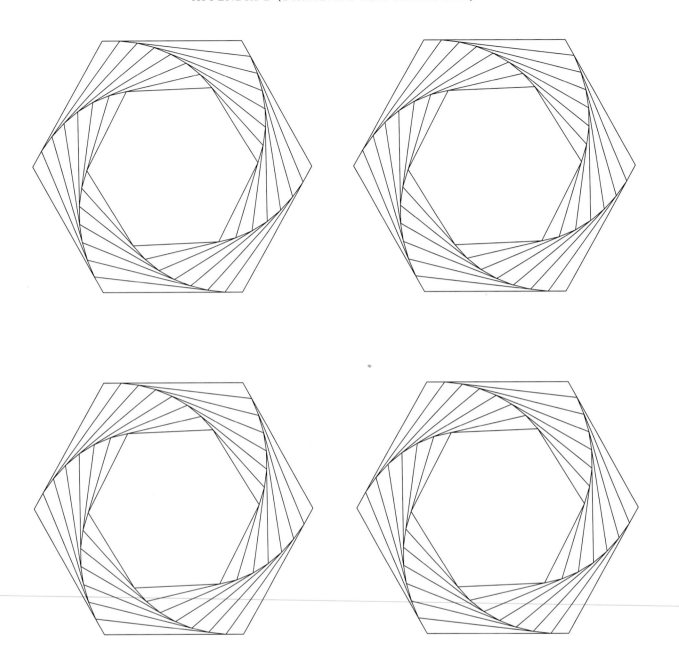

ABOVE
Reduced blocks of hexagons with a clockwise twist.

D3 DESIGN AND COLORING WORKSHEET

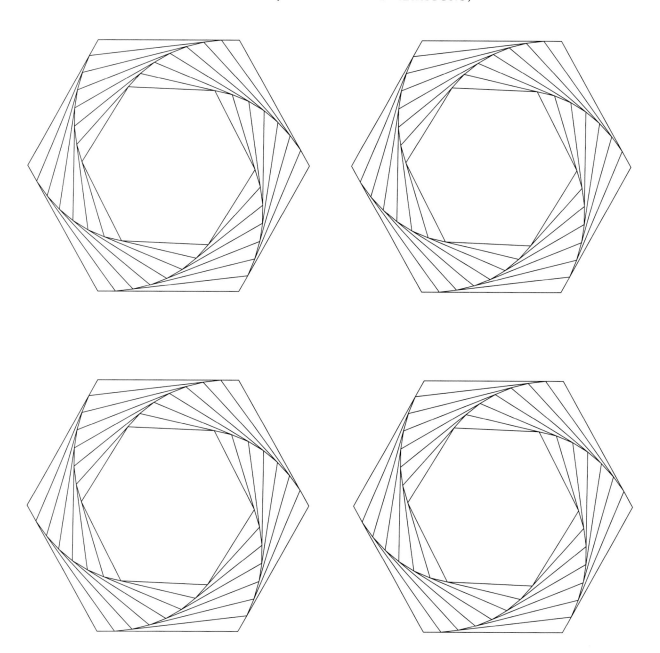

D4 DESIGN AND COLORING WORKSHEET

ABOVE
*Reduced blocks of hexagons
with a counterclockwise twist.*

∼ American Quilter's Society ∼
dedicated to publishing books for today's quilters

The following AQS publications are currently available:

- **Adapting Architectural Details for Quilts,** Carol Wagner, #2282: AQS, 1992, 88 pages, softbound, $12.95
- **American Beauties: Rose & Tulip Quilts,** Gwen Marston & Joe Cunningham, #1907: AQS, 1988, 96 pages, softbound, $14.95
- **Appliqué Designs: My Mother Taught Me to Sew,** Faye Anderson, #2121: AQS, 1990, 80 pages, softbound, $12.95
- **Appliqué Patterns from Native American Beadwork Designs,** Dr. Joyce Mori, #3790: AQS, 1994, 96 pages, softbound, $14.95
- **The Art of Hand Appliqué,** Laura Lee Fritz, #2122: AQS, 1990, 80 pages, softbound, $14.95
- **...Ask Helen More About Quilting Designs,** Helen Squire, #2099: AQS, 1990, 54 pages, 17 x 11, spiral-bound, $14.95
- **Award-Winning Quilts & Their Makers, Vol. I: The Best of AQS Shows – 1985-1987,** #2207: AQS, 1991, 232 pages, softbound, $24.95
- **Award-Winning Quilts & Their Makers, Vol. II: The Best of AQS Shows – 1988-1989,** #2354: AQS, 1992, 176 pages, softbound, $24.95
- **Award-Winning Quilts & Their Makers, Vol. III: The Best of AQS Shows – 1990-1991,** #3425: AQS, 1993, 180 pages, softbound, $24.95
- **Award-Winning Quilts & Their Makers, Vol. IV: The Best of AQS Shows – 1992-1993,** #3791: AQS, 1994, 180 pages, softbound, $24.95
- **Celtic Style Floral Appliqué: Designs Using Interlaced Scrollwork,** Scarlett Rose, #3926: AQS, 1995, 128 pages, softbound, $14.95
- **Classic Basket Quilts,** Elizabeth Porter & Marianne Fons, #2208: AQS, 1991, 128 pages, softbound, $16.95
- **A Collection of Favorite Quilts,** Judy Florence, #2119: AQS, 1990, 136 pages, softbound, $18.95
- **Creative Machine Art,** Sharee Dawn Roberts, #2355: AQS, 1992, 142 pages, 9 x 9, softbound, $24.95
- **Dear Helen, Can You Tell Me?...All About Quilting Designs,** Helen Squire, #1820: AQS, 1987, 51 pages, 17 x 11, spiral-bound, $12.95
- **Double Wedding Ring Quilts: New Quilts from an Old Favorite,** #3870: AQS, 1994, 112 pages, softbound, $14.95
- **Dye Painting!,** Ann Johnston, #3399: AQS, 1992, 88 pages, softbound, $19.95
- **Dyeing & Overdyeing of Cotton Fabrics,** Judy Mercer Tescher, #2030: AQS, 1990, 54 pages, softbound, $9.95
- **Encyclopedia of Pieced Quilt Patterns,** compiled by Barbara Brackman, #3468: AQS, 1993, 552 pages, hardbound, $34.95
- **Fabric Postcards: Landmarks & Landscapes • Monuments & Meadows,** Judi Warren, #3846: AQS, 1994, 120 pages, softbound, $22.95
- **Flavor Quilts for Kids to Make: Complete Instructions for Teaching Children to Dye, Decorate & Sew Quilts,** Jennifer Amor, #2356: AQS, 1991, 120 pages, softbound, $12.95
- **From Basics to Binding: A Complete Guide to Making Quilts,** Karen Kay Buckley, #2381: AQS, 1992, 160 pages, softbound, $16.95
- **Fun & Fancy Machine Quiltmaking,** Lois Smith, #1982: AQS, 1989, 144 pages, softbound, $19.95
- **Gatherings: America's Quilt Heritage** Kathlyn F. Sullivan, #4526: AQS, 1995, 224 pages, 10 x 8½, softbound, $34.95
- **Heirloom Miniatures,** Tina M. Gravatt, #2097: AQS, 1990, 64 pages, softbound, $9.95
- **Infinite Stars,** Gayle Bong, #2283: AQS, 1992, 72 pages, softbound, $12.95
- **The Ins and Outs: Perfecting the Quilting Stitch,** Patricia J. Morris, #2120: AQS, 1990, 96 pages, softbound, $9.95
- **Irish Chain Quilts: A Workbook of Irish Chains & Related Patterns,** Joyce B. Peaden, #1906: AQS, 1988, 96 pages, softbound, $14.95
- **Jacobean Appliqué: Book I, "Exotica,"** Patricia B. Campbell & Mimi Ayars, Ph.D, #3784: AQS, 1993, 160 pages, softbound, $18.95
- **Jacobean Appliqué: Book II, "Romantica,"** Patricia B. Campbell & Mimi Ayars, Ph.D, #4544: AQS, 1995, 160 pages, softbound, $18.95
- **The Judge's Task: How Award-Winning Quilts Are Selected,** Patricia J. Morris, #3904: AQS, 1993, 128 pages, softbound, $19.95
- **Log Cabin Quilts: New Quilts from an Old Favorite,** edited by Victoria Faoro, #4523: AQS, 1995, 128 pages, softbound, $14.95
- **Marbling Fabrics for Quilts: A Guide for Learning & Teaching,** Kathy Fawcett & Carol Shoaf, #2206: AQS, 1991, 72 pages, softbound, $12.95
- **Mola Techniques for Today's Quilters,** Charlotte Patera, #4514: AQS, 1995, 112 pages, softbound, $18.95
- **More Projects and Patterns: A Second Collection of Favorite Quilts,** Judy Florence, #3330: AQS, 1992, 152 pages, softbound, $18.95
- **Nancy Crow: Quilts and Influences,** Nancy Crow, #1981: AQS, 1990, 256 pages, 9 x 12, hardcover, $29.95
- **Nancy Crow: Work in Transition,** Nancy Crow, #3331: AQS, 1992, 32 pages, 9 x 10, softbound, $12.95
- **New Jersey Quilts – 1777 to 1950: Contributions to an American Tradition,** The Heritage Quilt Project of New Jersey; text by Rachel Cochran, Rita Erickson, Natalie Hart & Barbara Schaffer, #3332: AQS, 1992, 256 pages, softbound, $29.95
- **New Patterns from Old Architecture,** Carol Wagner, #3927: AQS, 1995, 72 pages, softbound, $12.95
- **No Dragons on My Quilt,** Jean Ray Laury with Ritva Laury & Lizabeth Laury, #2153: AQS, 1990, 52 pages, hardcover, $12.95
- **Old Favorites in Miniature,** Tina Gravatt, #3469: AQS, 1993, 104 pages, softbound, $15.95
- **A Patchwork of Pieces: An Anthology of Early Quilt Stories 1845-1940,** complied by Cuesta Ray Benberry and Carol Pinney Crabb, #3333: AQS, 1993, 360 pages, 5½ x 8½, softbound, $14.95
- **Precision Patchwork for Scrap Quilts, Anytime, Anywhere…,** Jeannette Muir, #3928: AQS, 1995, 72 pages, softbound, $12.95
- **Quilt Groups Today: Who They Are, Where They Meet, What They Do, and How to Contact Them – A Complete Guide for 1992-1993,** #3308: AQS, 1992, 336 pages, softbound, $14.95
- **Quilter's Registry,** Lynne Fritz, #2380: AQS, 1992, 80 pages, 5½ x 8½, hardbound, $9.95
- **Quilting Patterns from Native American Designs,** Dr. Joyce Mori, #3467: AQS, 1993, 80 pages, softbound, $12.95
- **Quilting With Style: Principles for Great Pattern Design,** Gwen Marston & Joe Cunningham, #3470: AQS, 1993, 192 pages, hardbound, $24.95
- **Quiltmaker's Guide: Basics & Beyond,** Carol Doak, #2284: AQS, 1992, 208 pages, softbound, $19.95
- **Quilts: The Permanent Collection – MAQS,** #2257: AQS, 1991, 100 pages, 10 x 6½, softbound, $9.95
- **Quilts: The Permanent Collection – MAQS, Volume II,** #3793: AQS, 1994, 80 pages, 10 x 6½, softbound, $9.95
- **Roots, Feathers & Blooms: 4-Block Quilts, Their History & Patterns, Book I,** Linda Giesler Carlson, #3789: AQS, 1994, 128 pages, softbound, $16.95
- **Seasons of the Heart & Home: Quilts for a Winter's Day,** Jan Patek, #3796: AQS, 1993, 160 pages, softbound, $18.95
- **Seasons of the Heart & Home: Quilts for Summer Days,** Jan Patek, #3761: AQS, 1993, 160 pages, softbound, $18.95
- **Sensational Scrap Quilts,** Darra Duffy Williamson, #2357: AQS, 1992, 152 pages, softbound, $24.95
- **Show Me Helen...How to Use Quilting Designs,** Helen Squire, #3375: AQS, 1993, 155 pages, softbound, $15.95
- **Somewhere in Between: Quilts and Quilters of Illinois,** Rita Barrow Barber, #1790: AQS, 1986, 78 pages, softbound, $14.95
- **Spike & Zola: Patterns for Laughter…and Appliqué, Painting, or Stenciling,** Donna French Collins, #3794: AQS, 1993, 72 pages, softbound, $9.95
- **The Stori Book of Embellishing: Great Ideas for Quilts and Garments,** Mary Stori, #3929: AQS, 1994, 96 pages, softbound, $16.95
- **Straight Stitch Machine Appliqué: History, Patterns & Instructions for This Easy Technique,** Letty Martin, #3903: AQS, 1994, 160 pages, softbound, $16.95
- **Striplate Piecing: Piecing Circle Designs with Speed and Accuracy,** Debra Wagner, #3792: AQS, 1994, 168 pages 9 x 12, hardbound, $24.95
- **Tessellations and Variations: Creating One-Patch & Two-Patch Quilts,** Barbara Ann Caron, #3930: AQS, 1994, 120 pages, softbound, $14.95
- **Three-Dimensional Appliqué and Embroidery Embellishment: Techniques for Today's Album Quilt,** Anita Shackelford, #3788: AQS, 1993, 152 pages, 9 x 12, hardbound, $24.95
- **Time-Span Quilts: New Quilts from Old Tops,** Becky Herdle, #3931: AQS, 1994, 136 pages, softbound, $16.95
- **A Treasury of Quilting Designs,** Linda Goodmon Emery, #2029: AQS, 1990, 80 pages, 14 x 11, spiral-bound, $14.95
- **Tricks with Chintz: Using Large Prints to Add New Magic to Traditional Quilt Blocks,** Nancy S. Breland, #3847: AQS, 1994, 96 pages, softbound, $14.95
- **Wonderful Wearables: A Celebration of Creative Clothing,** Virginia Avery, #2286: AQS, 1991, 184 pages, softbound, $24.95

These books can be found in local bookstores and quilt shops. If you are unable to locate a title in your area, you can order by mail from AQS, P.O. Box 3290, Paducah, KY 42002-3290. Please add $2 for the first book and 40¢ for each additional one to cover postage and handling. (International orders please add $2.50 for the first book and $1 for each additional one.)

LOG CABIN
with a
TWIST

Barbara T. Kaempfer

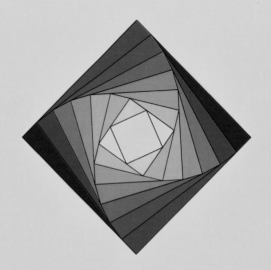

Born and raised in the capital city of Switzerland, the medieval tov of Bern, Barbara now lives with her husband, Ueli, in Mettmenstetten, a rur village halfway between Zurich and Lucerne. Their two children are grown and live in other towns in Switzerland.

Log Cabin with a Twist is Barbara's first book about quiltmakin She has been making and showing quilts since she first came to know th artful craft in 1982. At that time she was living with her family in Raleig NC, where her husband worked for three years on a professional assignment

After her family's return to Switzerland in 1985, she started teachir various quilting techniques in Swiss quilt guilds and shops. Since 1991 sl runs her own annual quilting seminar in the little Swiss town of Unterage and teaches the Log Cabin with a Twist technique to an international aud ence with great success. She is also a frequent guest teacher at seminars other European countries and the USA.

Barbara's work won numerous blue and red ribbons in internation competitions. Several articles have been published about her and her work the local and international trade press. Her mother tongue is Swiss-Germa she is fluent in German and English and understands French.

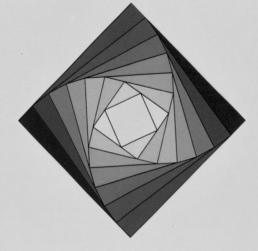

American Quilter's Society

P. O. Box 3290 • Paducah, KY 42002-3290

ISBN 0-89145-855-7

51895